Can I Tell You A
Secret?

A life's journey from victimization to victory as a survivor of extreme childhood abuse

Caroline Judd

Emerge Publishing Group, LLC
Riviera Beach, FL
www.emergepublishers.com

Library of Congress Control Number:
2010930274

ISBN 978-0-9825699-5-5

Published by
Emerge Publishing Group, LLC
Riviera Beach, Fl
www.emergepublishers.com

Caroline Judd, 2010
Can I Tell You A Secret? Caroline Judd
1. Autobiographical. 2. Inspirational.
3. Christianity

All scripture quotations, unless otherwise indicated are
taken from the Holy Bible, King James Version®

Printed in the United States of America

Acknowledgements:

Adriene Reid, sister . . .

You encouraged me to write down all the messed up stuff that I went through in life. You encouraged me to write a letter to all the persons who did me harm and even if I didn't mail it the weight of it all would be lighter and I would not be so burdened with my past.

Rachel Judd, niece . . .

You always told me to tell about my past. You cried with me when I cried and laughed with me when I laughed. You made me want to write and open up and tell it all.

Ben Stevenson, nephew and
Chiquita Smith, daughter . . .

The two of you stayed on me. You played a large part in keeping my spirits up. You wouldn't let me give up. You encouraged me to share with others who may be going through some trying times.

Joshua Judd, nephew . . .

Joshua, you are gone, but not forgotten. You always asked me, "Auntie, how is our book coming along?" It is finished. To God be the glory for all things.

Dedication

This book is dedicated to my husband and my friend for over twenty-five years and counting. Michael Judd has been known to keep God as the head of our all in all. He has never said to me, "You can't do that," instead he has encouraged me to start the task and challenged me to finish it.

Contents

Introduction

For a long time now I have been putting off this project. For whatever reasons I have stayed away from the topic of me. Maybe I was afraid of what would come from this. You know how people say "Let sleeping dogs lie" or "If it ain't broke, don't fix it." I don't know where folks get this stuff from. But I know one thing for sure, you just keep on living and I promise you some of the same old sayings will come to you.

I know what you are probably saying. "We all had it bad coming up." And you know, you are right. But I have learned that the old saying, "that if it don't kill you, it will only make you stronger," is not true. Whoever came up with this needs to stop the madness. Do you know that there are some people out in the world who are about to snap at the least little thing. Now there is a good saying for you, "that you never know which straw will be the one that breaks the camel's back." If you don't believe me just turn on your TV. You will not have to look long or hard.

I promise you some of the stuff people are doing these days, you would think you are watching a movie or something. It's funny how one day a person can go to work and one thing go wrong and wham bam, next thing you know the dude kills everybody that showed up for work that day.

You don't know how many folks are just trying to keep it together. Some people don't even know that they are ticking time bombs.

When I can find peace in words I try to keep them. Maybe I could pass them on to someone else who is trying to go through life as well, you know trying to keep it together. I would like to share some of them with you.

In regards to God's calling, do not be ashamed of your calling, nor should you be ashamed of the training that is needed to prepare you for God's calling. For if we are ashamed of him, come judgment time God will disown us. For the learning that is required of us today is for the souls of today and tomorrow. Not yesterday's souls. There is a higher and more advanced learning needed of God's chosen ones. So when God calls on us and prepares a way and even opens a door or two, for the edifying of his words, we should be glad and honored that God has answered our prayer. To be used by him is an honor. Do not ask for something and feel that you must keep it a secret as if you are ashamed of the gospel. We as children of God must learn to recognize when our prayers are being answered.

Always remember: To God be the glory.

A talebearer revealeth secrets; but he that is of a faithful spirit concealeth the matter.

Proverbs 11: 13

CHAPTER 1

Can I Tell You A Secret?

C an I tell you something, and don't tell anybody, OK?

On a hot summer day in 1972, I was nine years old. I can still smell the tart wine-like scent to this very day. I was lying on a twine bed crying and vomiting. I had been awaken by a large hand over my mouth, and the other hand pulling off my under pants. This hand was even bigger when balled up into a fist, and the voice that came along with it was deep and strained.

"Hush, before I really give you something to cry about."

As he climbed on top of me, he stretched my legs so far apart it made me feel as though I was being torn apart.

"It will all be over real soon."

I could feel the force in his hips as he kept trying to make that giant thing of his go inside of me. I remember thinking to myself that it won't fit so he has to stop. But no such luck. He just kept pushing and sweating. I could feel my body giving and something hot started to run down my legs. At first I thought I had peed on myself, but it hurt as though I was being stabbed with a knife.

"This could have been over by now if you would loosen up and let me finish before somebody walk in."

I prayed, "Dear God, let someone come and make him stop." Maybe I died or just passed out, because when I looked he was fixing himself.

"If you tell, I will come back and do it again and this time I won't stop until you are dead. Anyway, if you tell, no one will believe you. Oh, stop crying and get up and fix yourself up. You want everyone to know how fast you are?"

This man was my father's brother, yes, my uncle. He was the one who told me to let him know if anyone bothered me. And he would tell me "You know that you are just like my own, ain't nobody ever going to do you no harm, not around me, they won't."

I got up and did as he said, because I knew that somehow, this too, was my fault. As he got ready to leave the room, he looked as though he were speaking to someone else and said "You don't even know just how much I love you, do you?"

"All I am saying to you is that if I didn't do it someone else would have done it. Hell for all I know, one of your mama's old no good Negroes might have already done you. Do you know that them old guys kill young girls like yourself?"

And he pulled out a knife from his pants pocket, and said, "Usually I would have to cut me somebody to keep them from running their mouth. But that's how you can tell that I love you. Now get up and clean this mess up."

As I went about cleaning up, all I could think of was, if he loved me as he said, why was I hurting and being told not to tell anyone. No one would believe me anyway.

What was the part that no one would believe: that he loved me, or that he had just taken the only thing of value that I owned in life. And on top of that it was my fault that he had to do this to me. Not only had he just sexually molested me and threatened to cut and kill me, but he had the nerve to tell me that this was hurting him. He told me to keep all of this to myself. Who was I going to tell?

I never heard of anyone telling their parents anything as bad as this. First of all, my father wasn't even around to tell, and my mother always told me to stay out of grown up's faces.

Do you know that my parents never told us anything about who to come to if anyone tried to hurt us in any way, stranger nor family. I mean for all that I knew this was the first incident, or maybe nobody ever talked about it.

There's an old nursery rhyme called Humpty Dumpty. And as I went about the task of cleaning up, I can remember saying the words to myself, over and over again. "Humpty Dumpty sat on a wall Humpty Dumpty had a great fall, and all the king's men couldn't put poor Humpty Dumpty together again."

Maybe from way back then is when I started to count everything. As I walked from the back room I counted my steps, and as I stuffed the dirty sheets into a foot tub I counted how long that it took to fill up the foot tub with water.

As I sat on the toilet stool I could feel my under pants start to stick to me as if they were starting to become a part of me. There was so much blood. I had never seen that much blood come from one person. I wondered if this was all my blood, or did my father's brother bleed as well. From that day I made up in my mind that I was no longer going to call that man my uncle.

I promise you that I had to learn at an early age that bleach is not for all colors, because now I was in even more trouble for messing up the blue twin sheets. I believe that's where that old saying came into being, "If it ain't one thing it's another."

Yes, Humpty Dumpty did have a great fall. I had become that Humpty Dumpty. My life would no longer be the same no matter how hard I tried.

It would have helped to have someone to talk to, but there was never anyone around like that for me. You see no one talked with me about life. All I ever heard about was death, you know. I would hear statements like, " If you ever get too grown under my roof I will kill you." Or, "You must don't know who I am; I brought you into this world, and I damn sure will take you out."

Hey, sometimes she would even say to me "Do you think anyone would even care if I killed you. You are just another black child that the world has to deal with."

If it weren't for her I would have been dead and gone a long time ago. My Step-mom would say to me don't nobody want you; all you are, is just another mouth to feed. Even your no-good father don't want you. She told me this so much that I no longer looked up to my dad. I would see him and would go the other way with my head held down.

I remember a while back in the fall of the school year, when some of our cousins would stand at the bus stop and the older cousins would be talking with each other about sex, and boys, and periods. That is as close as I got to the lessons of life.

One of the older cousins said that if you start bleeding down there, that means you have been "doing it" with a boy and you are going to get pregnant. And no one will want their kids around you. Even the grown-ups will not want you around them. My cousin Nora knew a girl that this happened to. To this day that girl has not been seen.

So now here I am bleeding down there. My mama had already said that too many grown folks can not stay in one house.

"This is my house and I'm the only grown-up that's going to live in this house."

Although I was bleeding down there, I knew I had not let any boy touch me. All I know was that I had to hide this blood so that no one could know. If my sisters found out they would tell just as sure as I am standing here today. Hey, my two sisters, Mookie and Meme wanted nothing more than to see me dead. As if I didn't have enough trouble in my life without this added to it.

I got an old tube sock and some toilet paper and wrapped it, and then stuffed it into my underwear. I didn't know how much longer I was going to be able to keep this going. I didn't even know if I was going to bleed to death or have a baby. All I know was that if my mama found out I was as good as dead already.

I not only had to hide the fact that my father's brother had just raped me, but to add to this mess, now I'm bleeding.

And on top of that I have bleached mama's sheets. I don't care who sleeps on them or whatever it was, if it is under her roof it belongs to mama. And I promise you this woman could remember as far back as to when she was born. Sometimes I think she could remember when her mama was a child.

Of course, I could never tell her that because if you corrected her on anything, you had better get ready to pick up your teeth off the floor. So now you see why I couldn't throw the sheets away. Just my luck I would be putting it in a bag or trash can and someone would see me at the trash can. No matter if they saw me put anything in it or not all would be said is it was in the trash can and I was by the trash can. You know how black folks are, putting one and one together. It is a wonder I didn't crack up!

For real, I was trying not to get caught. Some time I would say now if she really want to do something for me she could just do it, you know kill me and be done with it. Stop trying to put fear into me, because at this point I was no longer afraid of dying. By now I truly did believe that death could be the best thing for me. I put the sheet into a shopping bag, and pushed it under the bed as close to the wall as possible.

I thought that I had it all figured out: first hide the sheet, then keep up with how many times that I would change my under pants. I know that I could not put them in the dirty clothes hamper. Nor could I keep trying to wash the same pair out, and then wear them over. My mama would most definitely know. That woman could have been a detective, or one of those CSI people, you know the people who catch the killers who leave bits and pieces of evidence behind. That woman would make Columbo look like yesterday's news.

It took some years to find out how she found out all that she knows. First, she would go through your clothes at the beginning of the week, and then again in the middle of the week. By the end of the week she could tell you everything you wore that week. And she knew just how not to disturb anything in a person's belongings. That woman didn't trust anybody.

It's funny now looking back, because she wanted everyone to trust and believe her. And she would always say that she would only trust a person only as far as she could throw them.

So now I have come up with the idea to wear my under pants for a couple of days, wash them and put them into the dirty clothes. Now she wanted to know why my under clothes were wet. I tell you, I couldn't win for losing.

I use to wonder when she had time to do all of this spying, only to find out that my sisters "Mookie" and "Meme" were spies on duty. I promise you what those two didn't see, they made up. I spent more time trying to get out of their mess than I did getting into my own mess. I don't believe those two even had childhood friends. My mom would treat them as if they were special. Now that I am grown up I see that she was right; sometimes special means slow.

So now I am in trouble for the wet under clothes, OK. I said to myself, just don't change them at all. And this, too, was not one of the best ideas that I came up with. If you must know the truth of the matter, it was not very bright at all.

Someone once said to me that "Association brings on assimilation." Yep, I had been around my dizzy sisters so long until I had actually become as dumb as they were.

Do you know that after a couple of days this odor started getting stronger and stronger until even I started to think that something was dead. I don't know about you, but when we were coming up we didn't have air conditioning, or ceiling fans. We had only one or two fans for the whole house. So that meant that somebody was not going to sleep under a fan.

Meanwhile the smell was growing worse by the day. I had to do something. I don't know exactly when it happened, but the bleeding stopped. I buried those underpants and the tube sock out in a field not far from our house. What a relief. Just knowing I was going to live another day was good enough for me.

Just when I started to think I had this thing licked, how about I started to bleed again. Stuff like this only happens to me. I tell you the truth, I didn't even know enough to call it what it was: my monthly period.

Instead of my mother telling me what was going on with my body, all she said was "If there is something you need to tell me about, you need to do so and be quick about it."

Now please, what was I going to tell her? "Oh, by the way I have been bleeding down in my private area, and I haven't been with any boy, but Uncle Lee hurt me down there until I started to bleed. And he said you wouldn't believe me if I told you. He also said he would come back to kill everyone."

I felt that since she was always probing and playing detective that she should already know, after all it happened under her roof. I used to try to stay off to myself. I felt that if anyone got too close they would find out, or I might say a bit too much and I couldn't allow this to happen.

I spent most, if not all, of my free time trying to make this thing go away. Out of all the things that I did, I would not even ask someone outside of the house about my problem.

During the course of that summer my father's brother molested me every chance he got. Whenever I found out he was going to be in town, I would do everything I could not to get trapped in the same room with him.

On some occasions I was allowed to spend the night with my father. That turned out to be just as nerve wracking. My father would bring us to his house and question me, my two sisters, and my brother.

"Who is staying in the house with y'all? How does your mom spend the money that I give her? Where does she get money from when I don't give her money?"

Then he would pull me aside and say, "One of these days you are going to find out about that crazy b#*#* and everything will finally make some sense to you."

I remember asking my father if I could stay with him and never go back home. He told me that now's not a good time; wait and see what will come through for him. He said he was working on something big, and if it went well we would be well off. As you may have guessed, it never happened.

He had a lady friend. We were never allowed to say "girlfriend" or "boyfriend" cause that would be too much like grown folks business, and for that kind of talk you would find yourself getting up off the ground. Now my father's lady friend would try to be nice to us and ask us things about ourselves. She seemed alright, I guess. Mama warned us not to go over there running our mouths about anything, because she was the boss, and no one runs her house but her. What happened in her house stays in her house.

My dad's lady friend said something odd to me one day.

"You remind me so much of your mother, it's scary. When was the last time you saw her?"

I was like what in the world is this nut talking about? I mean like did I not just come from home! I wondered where did my father find her?

I didn't know it at the time, but she was not crazy. She was trying to tell me something. Nevertheless, at that time all I saw was a mad person. And I really did need to stay clear of her.

One night I overheard her talking with my father.

"There is something wrong with that oldest girl of yours. I can't put my finger on it, but she is not well at all."

"What do you mean? Are you saying that she is sick or that she is not right in the head? "

"Both."

"I believe that is the best she can do considering who she is living with," my father said.

Miss Lady tells him that he should get me from around there cause if it was one of her children she would die and go to hell for hers. I always wonder why people would not just say that they would die for their kids, you know, but also go to hell for them.

My father said to her that if he tried to get only me that my mama would not go for that, she would make him take us all. And he just could not do that. He said that it would give her time to run the streets, and to become an even bigger whore than she was.

I went and got my other sisters so that they could hear what was being said. I didn't know that another world war would break out after that, but as soon as we got back home that Sunday night Meme told my mama. And she called me in the room and told me to tell her everything. And me not wanting no trouble made up something different. I said that we were told not to go back and to repeat anything that was said in their house. And my mama smacked me down and busted my top lip

"You better tell me right now, you little B##$%, just what they were saying over there."

So I told her all that had been said. That crazy woman became even crazier. She loaded us all into her car and went back over to my father's house. And when I tell you that she raised holy hell, I do mean just that. She cursed and swore to God that she was going to have to kill somebody for being in her business.

All three of them started to fight. I can't tell you who broke the fight up, but when we got back home I got a whipping for lying about my father saying that what's said in his house stays in his house.

Have you ever done something wrong and you knew that it was wrong, but it was to put an end to something even worse than the first wrong. Only to have it all blow up into your face. Yep, this was one of my many not so bright ideas that would come back and as they say bite me in the butt.

Several weeks had passed and my father's brother had gone back to wherever it was that he came from, some place down south. One of the grown-ups said he would not be back until the summer.

By now I had became ill; my skin did not even look the same. What do you do when the pain is so bad that you can't even tell where you're hurting at, when every part of your body is hurting. To add to all of my pain I had this horrible odor. I promise you that it is true that nobody should have to tell you that you have body odor, or in my case a bad odor. I know that other folks could smell me, yet nobody ever said anything about it.

When I was forced to be around other people, I would be uneasy and never let my guard down always looking to see if anyone was saying anything about my body odor, especially when I would be in a closed area. I can't believe that everyone just wanted to mind their own business, when everything a person said or did everyone in town would know about it. God forbid if a grown-up said what you had done. You couldn't even tell your side of the story. The first thing would be said is that you were calling a grown-up a liar. God help us all if this is what you were saying. You would find yourself either looking for what was left of your teeth, or try to clear your head of all the stars that you were seeing and I don't mean movie stars either. So, do you see where I am coming from?

Now after all of my creative thinking my mama might not even have to kill me. I was doing it for her and didn't even know it. I had gotten so sick that I started passing out, and whenever I went to the bathroom I would leave such a bad odor that whoever came in after me would say that someone needs to clean up the bathroom because something was dead in there.

I started sweating all the time and I just hurt all the time. Finally one day in school one of my teachers sent me to the nurse's office. The nurse asked all sorts of questions about menstruation and had I started yet. She said that I had a fever and that my heart was reacting.

And for all of the tea in China I didn't know what she was talking about. So not to look dumb or anything I just said "yes" to everything. She kept asking questions. I just wanted to get out of there before she needed me to take a note home to be signed or even worse before she needed to call my mama. I either said yes or "I am not sure about that." She sent me to lie down for a while; I was now trapped. I didn't know what was going to come of this and how it all was going to go down.

Within an hour I heard my mom's voice. If I wasn't sick and already close to death, she would make sure that the job was finished. That old nurse told her everything. I could hear what was being said and I tell you the truth I didn't know whether to cry or pray or just to try to escape. I don't know where to go, just not to be there, you know.

No such luck. My mom stuck her head around the curtain and said to me, " Bring your a*#* on here."

I knew that this was going to be the day of my death for sure, so to get my two cents in or my final words before death I said to the nurse "It's been nice knowing you and I wish that it didn't have to end this way."

When we left the school my mom took me to the family doctor. Would you believe me if I told you that my troubles were just beginning? The doctor told my mom that I had an infection in my blood and that some folks are born with it and others come by it from sexual intercourse. It was called STD.

Right then and there my mother hit me so hard that I went flying across the examining table. She cursed me out and said that I needed to be dead somewhere away from around her. The doctor threatened to call the police on her if she didn't get control of herself. And then he helped me off the floor and checked to see if I needed stitches or any other help from him.

"I knew you were never going to be nothing but bad news for anyone around you. You make black people look bad."

As I sat in the back seat of the car on the way home I don't know what all my mom didn't say to me. All I knew was I had no idea what I had done to get this thing. I didn't even know what it was. All of a sudden I started to feel glad that whatever it was, it was bad enough to kill me. I believed that this was the last thing that she would be able to whip me for. Yes, I was happy for this thing because no one could ever hurt me again.

It's seems so strange now when I think back on that time in my life, all I ever talked with God about was death and waiting to die. I would pray for death for Christmas, for my birthday, for summer break from school, and for every holiday.

For so many years I meditated and prayed to God to just let me die because to die would let me know that he heard and saw what I was going through. I prayed that God would love me enough to deliver me from all the hurts and troubles of this life. I believed that this Almighty God who could do all things, even he didn't care for me.

Now today I find myself praying for life, and to have it more abundantly. For as long as I can remember I have had a relationship with God, not a good one but nonetheless still a relationship.

When I got home I was asked how and when and where did this happen. All I could say was I don't know, and I did nothing, and it must have just happened in my sleep or something.

I am sure by now you know what happened. If no one ever told you anything about life and what to look forward to if you did a certain thing then this and that will happen to you. And you would probably deserve it if you willingly did it, you know what I am saying?

As my mom beat me she, she said "This type of stuff don't happen in my house."

"Who was it? What 'so-and-so' boy have you had up in here?"

And as usually all I could say was I do not know what she wanted me to say. And this was not a lie, because I had not been anywhere with nobody. And if I had told her about my uncle and what had happened with him she would have just said that I was lying. And any way that had been so long ago, how could that be where it had come from? Just think how I felt. I didn't know because she had not had the talk with me, but she said that she was going to beat me until I told her what she wanted to know.

And as she would hit me she would tell me to shut up making all that noise and tell her before she kills me, because dead is where I needed to be. I don't know who wanted me dead more, her or me.

At times, it seems as though life as I knew it would come to an end. But life only got worse. I know by now you are probably saying how could my life get any worse than it already was? I can tell you, it did.

All of my life it seems as though one rotten thing happened right behind each other. My mom would call me stupid and she called her sisters and would tell them how dumb she thought I was. From my point of view she was the dumb one because she never thought anything through.

She was the type of person who would not tell you anything or let you go anywhere; yet, she wanted you to have all the answers to life. During those days, they did not teach sex education in school, especially grade school. Who would have thought that grown-ups were looking at little kids as if they were grown-ups. No one ever talked about the perverts and the pedophiles out there, and the bad part about it is that a lot of the time it is not even other people, but the men folks in your own family.

In today's age, we tell our little ones what to do if someone touches them inappropriately, and what to do if a stranger comes near them. As a matter of fact we start telling them as soon as we think they are old enough to understand what we are saying to them.

How far back can you remember when you were coming up, that you would hear of someone doing something to a kid? And when you did hear of it you would always say that they must have been white. But do you know it happened, but folks just didn't talk about it. I believe that it happens in one out of every five families.

After all this happened I had to be put on medication. I was still having problems with my cycle. I would bleed so much that I messed up everything I wore and sat on. And don't let me be in bed when it started, all the sheets and mattress would be soaked all the way through. And I would be so weak sometimes and so sick that I would throw up. The doctor told my mom that I could not continue on like that. He said that I was anemic and would end up bleeding to death. See, there goes that word "death" again.

I didn't look for trouble, but trouble found me. I mean my luck was so bad that if someone was selling a raffle ticket and I was the only one who bought one I would still lose. There was an old hillbilly show that use to come on and there was a singer name Roy Clark and he would sing a song that said "If it weren't for bad luck I'd have no luck at all." Some time it was as if I would roll right out of one thing right into another. I mean like have you ever seen a person dodge a bullet only to get hit by train or a bus or something else, this is the kind of childhood I had.

For as long as I have known myself I had always believed that bad stuff happens to good people, and that good things happen to bad folks. I know better now, but think back on your life and see if it is just my way of thinking. Every bad and no-good person that you may have known, they seem to have an over flow of good luck, right?

You look up and here comes Mister No-good with a new car or here comes Miss No-good with a new outfit. Mr. No-good won't work for all the tea in China; but he is always dressed to kill, driving his big fancy car, and playing the role as the big spender.

Then you see Mister Good-doer who works from sun up to sunset. This fellow can't make ends meet for nothing; he has to rob Peter to pay Paul. And when you see him he can't even afford to drive around town nor can he spend his hard earned money on things he wants, only on things he needs.

I tell you that with all of this going on who could keep any kind of secret.

Wisdom is the principal thing; therefore
get wisdom: and with all thy
getting get understanding.
Proverbs 4:7

Solomon my son, whom alone God hath chosen, is yet young and tender, and the work is great: for the palace is not for man, but for the Lord God.
1 Chronicles 29:1b

CHAPTER 2

No, Life Is Not Like A Box Of Chocolates

There is an old nursery rhyme that says Humpty Dumpty sat on a wall, Humpty Dumpty had a great fall. And all the king's horses and all the king's men couldn't put poor Humpty together again.

It was during this period of abuse that I started to count everything, and I do mean everything. I would count how many steps it would take to leave a room so that the next time I could use less steps.

I remember once my step-mom said to me "Why do you breathe so loud?" Whenever I had to be anywhere close around her I would try to control how many times I would have to breathe. It got to the point where I got quite good at it. She accused me of trying to creep up on her.

"Make some noise when you come into a room." I was so into counting things that I started adding things up and dividing and multiplying stuff in my head. I got so good at it that I could do just about any kind of math problem in my head. I know you might be thinking, "How can this be a problem?" Right? Well, this became a big problem in school.

I remember one time in grade school I was asked to go to the board to do a math problem, so I went up and wrote the answer down but my teacher didn't want just the answer; she wanted me to show her how I got the answer. And I couldn't. I was accustomed to just seeing it in my mind and that was it. And for the life of me I could not show how I got the answer.

When I had to do home work my teacher thought that I cheated or got someone else to do my work. One day my teacher asked, "How can I believe you did the work when you can't show me how you got the answers?"

Every time she would call on me to do a problem, she would start marking my work as incomplete. For the longest I really thought that this teacher had it in for me. Every day it seemed like she would ask who wanted to do some math problems on the black board and I promise you I never did raise my hand and she would call on me as if I had raised my hand. I would go up to the black board and wait for her to start her anguishing persecution.

It seemed as though instead of being in school I was in a courtroom or being executed. This went on daily. It seemed as though I was there to entertain my teacher or something.

No matter how many times she would call me up and put a math problem on the blackboard I would do the math in my head and then write the answer down

"How do you know the answer is right," she asked.

"Because I feel that it is."

"Well, show me so that I can see that you are right." When I could not show her, she would send me to the corner and the other children would be her audience. No matter what she said they would laugh.

I really did learn to hate at an early age. I use to call them the big dumb ape and her little stupid monkeys. I know that hate is a bad word for a kid to use, but any individual who is being tormented, whether they are young or old, the word hate will raise its ugly head. And being a kid with no one to explain to you what is happening, what else can I say?

After this went on for a month or more, I decided to tell her why I believed that she didn't know if my answers were right or not. Now I must tell you that this was not one of my brighter moments. No, not even close to being bright at all. Now I did feel good afterwards. In fact, it was like an outer body experience, like I was listening to someone else tell her off.

When I tell you that all hell had broken loose, you don't know the half of it. That woman grabbed me by my arm and dragged me out the classroom and up the hall and around the corner and up the stairs to the principal's office.

Now I know that the big guns were out. Yes, my mom would be called and from there a beat down would occur. I was going to get a beating for something this time. And I never said that I was a preacher's child, but I told that woman some stuff that day. I felt justified. And up until my mom got there I felt nothing else. She beat the fool out of me right there in front of my teacher.

She wasn't helping matters much. It was like she was promoting a big fight or something. Just when I thought my mom was through beating me, here goes my teacher and she told me to #*"**# and she told me to#*#*and she called me a you know what. So I said that's not what I said.

"Are you calling this nice lady a liar?"

"No, mom, you called her that."

She slapped me again. Then mom asked, "Why would this nice lady say this about you if it's not true?" That's when I told her and the principal everything she had been doing to me month after month. I told how she called me dumb and stupid and how she called me lazy and a cheater when I know that none of this was true about me. I told how she and the class would laugh and call me a little black lazy dazy who can't do my work.

This stopped the beating for a while and the other children were asked about it and they did confirm what I had said. I don't know what happened to that teacher because my mom cursed her out and I was sent out the office.

All I know was that I was put up a grade and did not see that teacher any more. It was some years later that I learned what little black lazy dazy meant. We were from the north and around that day and time being black was nothing to be singing about being black and proud. We only had "I am black and barely getting by." We were taught to say "yes ma'am and no ma'am, no sir and yes sir." Not just the little black kids but even the older folks would say this to the white folks.

I remember one summer we were with my grandmama working out in the tomato field. Some younger white people were out there and they were speaking to my grandmama as though she was a child or something as if she was not able to comprehend the bad and uneducated hillbillies conversation they were having. And all the while she was saying "yes sir" and "yes ma'am."

They had neither respect nor consideration that my grandmama was twice their ages. I couldn't understand why we had to show them respect at all times. And they didn't even have sense enough to talk to older folks with respect.

One time we were at a convenience store in Maryland. We were not allowed to all go into the store at once; we had to go in two at a time. Those folks would follow us all around the store saying "Can we help you people with something." Now the older kin folks would know what was going on, because they would say to us "Who want to make a quarter?" We would just about kill to do it. As kids, we didn't know that the folks in the store did not like black people, in fact we were hated and were none the wiser. We were like lambs to the slaughter.

When we got to the counter to buy our chips and snacks they would tell us how much to pay them and we would put our money in their hands and hold out our hands for our change only for them to throw it on the counter. We were told to always ask for a bag; that way you won't be called a thief. When we came out of the store we had to tell everything that happened.

Now that I think about it, the white folks did the older black folks wrong. And the older black folks did us younger black folk wrong. Ain't that nothin' for you. Wow, and I thought I was smart. Duh.

Now I don't want you to think that only white people were like that. There were black people who disliked other black people. Like my mom. If you didn't look at her closely, she could pass as a white person in the winter time. I mean she didn't have the "good" hair, but she would never be caught out and about without having on her wigs. It took me forever to come to the revelation that if you had the right color you could have it made.

I used to hear my dad say "If you are white, you just right and if you are brown, stick around but if you are black stand back." Some other folks would say that if you had light skin that meant that it was some cream somewhere in the coffee. And, oh yeah, I just heard dark skin folks saying this. And now I know what this means. If you had "good hair," Oh my God, it meant that you were part Indian. Now I don't know what part; maybe all of that royal crown had something to do with which part, you know.

I don't know what happened to my mom cause when she was home she would walk around us with no wig on and for her to be a grown-up she had the amount of hair as a little kid, rough and nappy and short. You know, like someone with a bad perm. Back in the days all we knew about was a straightening comb.

Mom walked straight at home. But whenever she saw men folks around, she suddenly became bow-legged. She would put her wig on and her black lip liner which was also her eye liner and her fake mole. We use to call her lipstick "prostitute red." Every man in town knew her. She would have you believe that was a good thing, but I never did like the way she acted to get attention from the men.

Now to this very day I can't comprehend why my mom disliked light skin black people. Either they were trying to be white or they thought they were better than everyone else. First of all isn't that what we all wanted, to be better then the next person. And if we didn't believe it then who would? And if you were a darker skin color she disliked you because you were trying to be somebody. I mean who in their right mind does not want to be someone?

I tell you this woman had no friends; she even went years without talking to her own mother and sister. And if she did not care for you we (the kids) were not allowed to speak to you either. There were six of us, three girls and three boys. Three of us had the same father and you can figure the rest out. For the longest we thought four of the six was my dad's. But after years of paying and missing child support payments and going to jail for eighteen years, my

father found out that one of my sisters wasn't his.
But get this: one of his good old friends from up
north turned out to be her father. Crazy, huh? Yeah,
I know.

I remember there was this one lady that was our
neighbor and was also supposedly a good friend of
my mom but it turned out that she was a better friend
to my dad. I don't know how my mom found out. It
was right after Christmas and we had toys
everywhere. My mom was sewing when my dad
came home. They had some words back and forth
and the next thing I see is my dad putting his fingers
in her face. I don't know where that razor blade
came from but my mom hit my dad across the hand
and blood flew everywhere.

They left together going to the hospital or
somewhere. All I know is that when they came back
my mom told me to get in there and clean up dad's
blood. Blood was all over the new toys, on the walls,
the floor, and the table. Everywhere you looked there
was blood.

"Mom, can someone help me?"

"No, you are his heart so I think his heart should
clean up his blood."

Every since that episode, my mom had no lady
friends. But she had men friends or rather new
"uncles." That's what we had, OK?

All I can tell you is black people are a strange
race of people, at least my family. I didn't know that
there was a group of words that would sum them up
like "hypocrite," "manipulative," and "dysfunctional"
They thrived off hurting each other. And when one
person got hurt it was like the end of the world. You

ever see someone so hurt till it was a shame. I mean you really felt bad for them. And the next thing you would hear, the hurt person was going around hurting someone else. And have you ever noticed they even have something just as cruel and hurtful as did the first person who hurt them. You know, like what goes around comes around. Or you know misery loves company. You know dumb stuff like that.

Now if I hurt and start to cry and my feelings have been hurt, I know that I am going to be looking pitiful as if I have been sucking on a real sour lemon or something. So why on God's green earth would I want someone that I call myself to love to feel the same way? And who in their right mind wants company when they're hurt? I know that when I am hurt I want to be alone and don't want to hear anything or see anything.

Have you ever cried so much till no noise or tears come out or your pillow gets soaking wet from the tears. I can remember crying so much and asking God to take me right now because I hurt too bad to get over what was going on. I'm not talking about the death of a love one or anything like that. I mean someone close to you says something to another person about you. And sometimes what they say may not even be true. And you know that it's not true but you carry on like the world was coming to an end, yes, a dumb mess.

And here is another one for you. You will hard down fight and get all banged up for them, even get a front tooth knocked out for this person today. By tomorrow you end up fighting and trying to knock their front teeth out.

I have come to believe that my family doesn't know how to love. Oh, we think we know but we don't. Let a cousin or a sister look at you the wrong way. And what is the wrong way? I don't believe that there is a right way. All we need to do is to see them getting into a car or walking in a store. If we feel they have looked at us the wrong way, it's on from there. We are ready for a throw down.

Everyone and their mom's mom know about what is going on except the other person that you are mad at. Sometimes the other person has not even seen you and more than likely don't even know what you are talking about. They can be minding their own business and just going about doing what needs to be done when all of a sudden someone come and let (him or her) know that some crazy loon is stalking them and wants to jump them. So what do we do? We act just as nuts as the other person trying not to look like a deer caught in a car's headlights. We tend to go a step further and show the whole world that we can be even more immature then the next person. We can carry on like this for years or even decades if it will make it seem as though we are the stronger one. Do you notice that we call the stronger person the one who is right.

You can be just as wrong as two left shoes, but because you beat up the other person that means you are the winner. I don't know how we associate the word "winner" with "right." And even if we lose the fight we will never admit it. We'll say that someone was holding me while the other person was free to fight. Or we'll say something stupid like, "You know, technically, I didn't lose I just didn't want to hurt nobody." Whether you establish who wins or not you are still home trying to put alcohol and band-aids on your scratched up knees. We wear sun glasses in the house to hide our black eye and try not to chew on the sore side of our mouth. I don't know if I have established how crazy my kin folks are. They call right wrong and wrong right. And can go around disliking a person simply because of the color of their skin.

I remember there was this girl at our church. Oh, you thought we didn't go to church. Yeah, we did go to church every Sunday morning. We called it mourning because that's what it felt like. It was an A.M.E. church that was so dead we kids would say we woke up to go to church to go back to sleep.

Now this young girl, I'm going to call her Robin, was tender eyed. Maybe she thought God said he was passing out books when He really said he was passing out looks. She declined his offer. I don't know what happened to the rest of the family, but they looked alright. Robin knew that folks were talking about her, not just the kids but even the grown-ups too. And she would stay off to the back of the church. Her sister would always be by her side no matter what was said about her.

Now when the holidays come the grown-ups would make all of the kids come to the front and recite a speech that they gave us. But I don't know how my aunt found out about it but Robin had herself a little secret. After all the kids had done their speech and everyone thought the program was over, my aunt calls Robin up to the microphone.

All eyes are on her and she drops her head and starts to cry. Her big sister goes to her, whispers something in her, pulls her head up and wipes her face with her hand. She hugs Robin, holds her hand and stands there with her.

By now, there is not a dry eye in the whole church. And then it happened. Robin starts to sing and the voice that comes from her is angelic. It's the closest thing we knew to Godliness.

And I tell you everybody's mouth was wide open. We were in shock and nobody said a single word not even the pastor. Afterwards, my aunt asked her sister what did she whisper in Robin's ear and she said "I told her that she was and is the most beautiful person in this building and to sing to the Lord not to the ugly acting people."

I can remember that everybody wanted to be friends with Robin after that. Out of all the years going to that church, the only lesson I learned was that beauty is only skin deep. You can be as good looking as you want to be but if you treat people nasty and your ways are ugly, your actions make you an ugly person. I learned that words can hurt. We used to say, sticks and stones may break my bones, but words will never hurt me not. Not so; this is one big lie that comes from the father of all lies.

I was told every day of my childhood life that I was ugly and black with big eyes. I was told that I would never amount to anything. I hated myself and had little or no self esteem. Because of that I hurt other people by saying hateful and ugly things to them. When I saw how hurt Robin was from being called all those nasty and hateful things, I decided not to ever make anyone feel bad ever again.

I believe that it is better to learn something late than to never learn at all. I have learned that it is unnecessary to cause pain to anyone just to try to make yourself feel big. It doesn't work; it only makes you look smaller. There is a word for this; it's called abuse.

I don't know if you know this or not but a person can be verbally abusive as well as physically abusive. I am speaking from both sides of the abused line because when you don't know any better that's all you've got. And yes, it's true that abused people become abusers as well. Studies have shown that at least 85% or more abused people become abusers.

I was able to see firsthand how words can hurt. When I saw the hurt on Robin's face, that was a wake-up call. Robin had done nothing but come to church like the rest of us. She only wanted to be left alone and have a bit of peace. We were the ugly ones for tormenting her.

You know that's bad when a person can't even find peace in the church. That is just wrong. Not one grown-up tried to stop us or try to correct us. But I thank God for showing me what hurt looked like. I started to cry when I saw the hurt look on Robin's face and it made me see myself. I thought of all the times I had been called black, big-eyes, stupid, dumb, and ugly. From day one I was being told that I was no good and that I was going to end up just like my no-good father. Whenever I said something hateful and hurtful I felt justified and taller for doing so, until God showed me myself though Robin's pain.

From that day I made it my business to change. Whenever I saw Robin I would smile and wave at her. She wouldn't wave back at first, but as time went on she started to come around. And if we got any treats or snacks I would not eat mine no matter how bad I wanted it. I would give mine to Robin and her sister. I felt like this was a way that I could stop some of the hurt that was in this world.

From that moment in my life I started to look people in the face whenever I talked to them. I started to think about what I would say and how I would say it before I said or did anything to anyone. I didn't know much back then but I did know that I didn't want to be the cause of anyone hurting.

Sometimes I would cry because someone had hurt my feelings. I felt like I needed to be the one who could stop the awful and nasty dialog that our family was doing.

I have been around people who it seems that every other word that comes out of their mouths is a curse word. And if they had to communicate without cursing they could not do it. The grown-ups do it and the children learn from them. Out of all the things that we should be learning, becoming a professional curser shouldn't be one of them. It is a shame when a young person can't express themselves without talking nasty and being rude.

So this does bring me to this conclusion: No, life is not like a box of chocolate because with the box of chocolate you already know what's in it. You know where to start and where to end. But with life all we can say is how well we remember our past and what we wish for our future. But there are two roads that we can take in life. Either we can walk with God or we can walk it alone.

This old journey of life may have started on a bumpy trail some years ago, not knowing whether the end would be near or fair, but through it all I have learned to lean and trust in God. It has taken me many years to seek God's will for me rather than my own will.

Even though I may weep some nights till my pillow is soaked, I do know that joy does come in the morning. It was never promised to me that every day was going to be sunshine, so if it's raining, I don't hold my head down. I have learned to look for a rainbow. And when it's sunny I still look up to the hills from which cometh my help.

Even so the tongue is a little member, and boasteth great things. Behold , how great a matter a little fire kindleth!
James 3:5

*Hatred stirreth up strifes: but
love covereth all sin.*
Proverb 10:12

*Greater love hath no man than this,
that a man lay down his life
for his friends.*
John 15:13

CHAPTER 3

Why Is It That His Love Has To Hurt?

For as long as I can recall whenever I would get a beating my mama would say "Do you think I like beating you? Don't you know that this hurts me," or "You act as if you are the only one here who is getting hurt." All I could think of was, is she for real?

You know I've always wondered why folks say stuff like that. Even when my uncle was molesting me he said to me, this was hurting him just as much. What kind of nonsense was this? I also remember one time my uncle was talking crazy stuff like he was out of his mind. Maybe he was drunk or high on something because he says to me "You know I will kill your whole family if you ever tell anyone." He said that he would get away with it because he was not going to do time for nobody not even his own mother.

So I said to myself, oh, like who is this guy talking to. Go on and kill them; they don't even like me and there is not a day that goes by that my mom wasn't talking about killing me. My sisters and brothers were like working for the poe poe (police). If I had done something they were going to tell it, and if I had not done anything, someone was going to make something up. Either way a whipping or a slap or a back hand was coming.

So you can see why I felt that, hey, uncle just do what you have to do like why should I have to go through this all by myself. It is not as if there was going to be any love lost, you know. I don't know why people always threaten kids with death whenever they do something wrong. It had gotten to the point where that's all was being said "I'm going to kill you." How do you work that into a conversation anyway? So I had heard this every-day all day. By now I just wanted them to stop talking about it and start doing it. At least there would bean end to the threats and we could start something different.

Sometime I would get mad at myself for not speaking up. I would think something to myself instead of just saying it. I mean, it's not like I wasn't going to get a whipping anyway. I would go around not saying what was on my mind, trying not to rock the boat. By not speaking up I was making myself sick with ulcers and getting gray hairs early in life. Meanwhile, everybody and their mama's mama are going around telling folks off and then suffering the consequence at a later time.

When I was still in grade school, I had gotten really sick. My mom finally got tired of the school complaining about me vomiting and nearly jumping out of my skin every time someone would get loud. So she finally broke down and took me to the doctor.

When she found out that it was going to take more than one day of her time in order to run some tests on me at a different doctor's office, she flipped her wig for real. I promise you we when went into the doctor's office, the part in her wig was in the middle. When she was told the news about having to take me to another doctor for more tests, her wig's part was on the side like she was wearing a flipover or something.

She informed me that something had better be wrong with me or else I would be coming back to the doctor for the whipping that she was going to put on me. If there was a way that I could have made myself feel better I would have done that from the get go. I mean, why on God's green earth would I have wanted to be left alone with her out of all the people in the world.

The test results came back and revealed that I had a nervous stomach which had turned into an ulcer. I was not able to hold anything on my stomach and I had lost a lot of weight. And to add to the matter I wasn't sleeping at night.

The first thing my mom had the nerve to ask the doctor: "Well, how did she catch that?" and "Can you catch it from her?"

"It's always one thing or another with her. I have five other children and I don't have trouble with none of them. She's just trying to get attention again.

Every time she does something like this, all I need to do is put her in her place and she will learn how to act."

When the doctor finally explained to her the cause of my sickness and what would be needed for me to get better, she had the gall to say that I was having problems in school and that she didn't know that it had gotten so out of hand. I couldn't believe the words that were coming out of her mouth.

He brought to her attention the bruises and scars that were on me. He read some of the other doctor's notes to her about how it had seemed that I was being abused by somebody on a regular basis. He put it on record that she had been informed about it. She still tried to say that it had to be happening at school. Oh, if you could have seen that woman acting like she was in shock or like someone could have knocked her over. She says that she blamed the school for everything that I was going through and that someone ought to go there and find out what was happening because it was no telling how many other kids was being abused there.

The doctor was looking at her like, is she for real, and she must have really believed what she was saying cause she started saying to me tell the doctor what happened when you was five.

"Mama, what are you talking about?"

"Don't be afraid. Go on and tell him some of the things that happened to you."

You remember all I could say was I don't know because this doctor looked as if he was going to call the law and have both of us thrown not in the jail but under it. And I did know one thing for sure and that was that I was not going to be on nobody's news paper front page for lying. No way, Jesus.

And out of all the whipping that I have gotten from telling lies whether I was lying or not all I know was mama hated a liar. She would say "If you lie you will steal and if you steal you will kill."

Now all of a sudden here she was trying to get me to lie for her. I couldn't believe the nerve of her. After all of her wheeling and trying to deal, the doctor told us both that child welfare was going to have to be called in so that they could establish what was going on. If they found foul play going on, the authorities would come and someone would be in a lot of trouble and could even go to jail.

Hey, that was all I needed to hear. I started to shake and before long I was about to toss my cookies right then and there. I thought that he was here to help. Now someone was going to jail. I had never been to a doctor like this before and I didn't want to be there any longer. From the looks of my mom she wanted out as well. She had one of those looks on her face like someone had been walking around with the bottom of their dress tucked in their panty hose and didn't know how long she had been walking around and who all had seen it.

Yeah, she didn't want to hear nothing else that man was talking about. And I think by now my mom had figured out that the doctor wasn't buying her story about the school and that she was a suspect. All that was running through my mind was that the power she supposed to have over men must not apply to men with all of their own teeth and that don't smell like a gutter. Or maybe she didn't have her mole colored in on the right side of her lip.

For whatever reason, he was not feeling her and I don't believe mama was pleased with that. So we needed to be somewhere else like yesterday. If you could have seen her trying to get out of there and to stop the doctor from telling her what all was going to happen and what types of medicines that was needed for the treatment.

She said to me "Go to the car and wait for me there and I will be right out."

And sure enough she did come running out soon after. All she said to me was that it turned out that this was the wrong kind of doctor after all and that she would give me a note for the school telling them to mind their own #*^# business and that they can kiss her #** and if they didn't like that she would take them to court and show them who she knew. She said that life was not what you know but who you know. I did everything that I could not to laugh at her because I know everybody she knew and nobody that we both knew would move on her behalf. If anything they would help the other side.

Nonetheless I said nothing trying not to wake her from whatever kind of trip she was on. All I knew at that moment that whatever she was on I wanted some and if she wasn't on anything then she did need something.

Not long after the trip to the doctor's office some people started coming to our house and life became miserable. All of us children were told what to say whenever someone asked us something. We were told not to volunteer any information to them. So if anyone came to the house when she wasn't there, we were not allowed to answer the door. She had to be there to make sure that no one would try to get us to tell any of her business. And whenever the family would ask her what was going on she had an answer for them.

"That girl got sick at school and now they want to make it seem that I'm the cause of it."

Not long after the doctor thing went down we had to come straight home after school and do all the house work and not come outside until my mama came home. She had us so confused that we didn't know if we were coming or going.

"Mama, who are we to look for?"

"White people," she said. "If anyone looks like that get in the house and don't make a sound."

I can just imagine how we must have looked to our neighbors. Every time someone white would drive up we would cut out like it was a matter of life or death. The crazy part about this plan was that we lived near a major highway that ran straight through white and black people's neighborhood. So at anytime someone white could be going home or even coming to see someone. All I know is we were running back and forth so much that we looked like little fugitives running from the law every time someone white came by.

After some weeks of running and ducking and hiding a black lady came up to us and started asking us questions.

"Do you live here? How many people live here? What happens when you get in trouble, do you get whippings or do you get put in time out?"

"We get put into headlocks until we pass out," said my older brother.

Right away the lady started writing in this little book. She asked how many times a day we get whippings. Everyone started to laugh and gave her different numbers. All of a sudden, she asked me. I told her I didn't know. One of my sisters said "too many."

"How many is too many?"

"She is the only person I know that gets a beating for waking up in the morning," my sister said.

Everyone burst out laughing and even the lady started to laugh like she was just an everyday person. She still wrote in her little book, like she was writing down some good jokes or something. So we kept on telling her what she wanted to hear.

When she had heard enough she just walked away and we thought nothing of it, until one of my little brothers said that lady was going to write about him because she liked him the best.

We thought that mama was not paying attention to our conversation. All of a sudden she slammed her plate.

"What the f#*! is he talking about? What lady? When did this happen? What did I tell you stupid little S O. B's?"

Oh, my God, she just cursed everybody in the house out. She had her front teeth out so it was kind of hard to understand everything that she was saying. Standing in front of her was not a good place to be, because she spat when she was talking. She was jerking back and forth and she had turned red in the face. Her little bit of hair was standing straight up on her head; she had more hair on the top than on the sides. This made her look like a rooster walking up and down the hallway.

We all took out running, everyone to their own hiding place and the best place to be right about then was far, far away cause life as we had known it was to be no more.

She was not going to stop her war on us until she had whipped the fool out of us all. Now what we tried to do was to neither be first to get caught nor the last. If you were first she would snap and no one knew how long she would be whipping you and if you were last she would just be catching her second wind and you got it worst.

If you got caught in the middle she would have to save her strength for the next kid and there were six of us and the only person that was safe was the baby. And that cat would be the main one who had been talking. And if we cried out that it was the baby who told everything, she would say you are older than him so you should have stopped him from running his mouth.

Now how were we to do that when she would always tell us to keep our hands off her baby.

"When you have children of your own then you can beat someone."

So how were we to stop the little imp (worker for the devil) from running his mouth? All he ever did was run his mouth from the time he learned how to talk. And the kid lived in a fantasy world. He never told the truth about anything. I mean don't get me wrong he was a lovable kid. But to love him was like trying to hug a rattlesnake. You know you're going to get bit but you don't know when.

So everyone's head were rolling around the house trying not to catch the bad end of the whipping deal. When she got to me she started hollering.

"Nobody is going to rip my house apart, do you hear me?"

She is one of those people who always says that she would die and go to hell if anyone ever messed with any of her kids, but she never ever did. Because according to my count she should have been gone at least three or four years ago.

Now I am trying to figure out what is she talking about now and how is this my fault. Have you ever got a whipping and all the while you are trying to talk your way out of the whipping only to find out that you don't even know what you did to deserve the whipping?

My mama was the type of person who would be asking you all different kind of questions the whole time that she is beating you. And when she would run out of things to ask, then she would start saying, "Now hush; shut up, do you hear what I am saying?" Now how can you hush up when she is still beating the fool out of you? And the more she beat you the louder you get and the crazier mama got.

About a month had gone by and we thought that all was clear with the D.C.F. people only to find out that the lady had come back. This time she brought another lady with her and at first sight of her we took off running. We grabbed our baby brother's hand, picking him up off his feet. All you could see was his feet moving and not touching the ground.

WHY IS IT THAT HIS LOVE
HAS TO HURT?

We got in the house, closed and locked the doors and windows. We turned off all the lights and just sat there waiting for the world to come to an end or whatever was to come next. The D.C.F. worker left a letter on our door and left. My older brother got it and read it and said, "If ya'll don't want another beating we need to throw this letter away" and we did. And at that time we thought the battle was over not knowing that it had only just begun.

The lady came back. This time my mom was at home. You could hear her hollering and cursing and calling those people liars and telling them what she was going to do to them if they didn't get off her property. We all came running to see what was going on.

"What in the hell is she talking about saying she left a letter here for me?"

"We don't know what's she's talking about."

Even the baby said, "Mama them people are telling you a big fat story and you need to whip them cause you hate that."

I think that was the one and only time that we all stuck together. Even though it was a lie, we stood there in front of mama and told the biggest lie ever and guess what our mom said to those ladies?

"You heard my children and they don't lie so get off my property."

I said to myself now who's lying? Because that's got to be the biggest lie ever told. And she had a straight face telling it.

I don't know how long the problem with them went on but I was glad when it was over cause all

that running and still taking all that medicines was
not good for my health.

My kin folks use to have a saying, "Don't let
nobody catch you slipping." And for the love of God
don't ever fall in love with anyone and let my family
get wind of it. If it's a guy then the first thing they
will say is "Oh, he is just using her just to get what
he want from her," and if it is a female "Oh, she is
just playing him; she got his nose wide open."

My family couldn't see the beauty in folks being
in love and just enjoying each other's company, so
when we found that someone special, we would
sneak around and hide and pray that no one from our
family would find out. Those people would make it
seem as though you were dating your cousin or an
alien instead of being happy for you and accepting
that person. And please don't hold your breath
waiting for them to welcome them to the family.
Man, I tell you by the time that my folks were
finished with your love ones, they and everyone else
would not be speaking to you and may even have a
restraining order out on you.

What's the name of that old school song? I don't
know if it's called "A Thin Line Between Love and
Hate" or if those are words were in the song. All I
know is love hurts in this family cause even the
grandparents will be saying, "Lord I don't know
what they see in them folks." Everybody's business
is everyone's business. Love does hurt; that's all I
can tell you.

I really do believe that is why we and when I say
we, I am not just talking about my family, but we as
a race of people are dysfunctional or you could even

say nonfunctional because we have not been educated on how to communicate with one another or how to invest into ourselves or each other. We do things because we feel like it and not because it is the right thing to do.

We have not been taught that it is better to help someone to be successful without having a spotlight on us. You know, the big I, and the little U, syndrome. Whenever we do something for each other, first we need to know what's in it for us or how is this going to make me look big. It hasn't been instilled in my family that we can make a difference in this world.

Now I don't want any of you getting upset with me and say that I am talking about you or anyone that you may know. This is why I say my family! Now if it turns out that you are in my family then the only thing that I can tell you is you know that I am not lying. Oh yeah and holler...

We don't have successful relationships with our spouses because we don't trust each other and we don't want to submit ourselves to our husbands because we feel that we are banking more and we bring more to the table then him. And we want him to come home and cook and clean and take care of the kids so that you can have some down time, and we don't like his friends cause they are all dogs.

Even though the Bible says that the man is the head of the woman and the home, we as young women (and some older women) feel a need to wear the pants in the family. And I know that you know me by now, well, enough to know that it's the men's turn now. You can have a good wife at home but you have to prove to your fellows that "you de man" so you cheat on her in every way that is possible; you don't bring home all of your pay to help with the bills and the kids.

You know, I see nowadays more men taking care of someone's kids than their own. You (the man) hurt your family and you disrespect your wife just to be called the man. And for you guys who call yourself on the "down low," Well players, that is a whole nother book and we won't be putting it out there for you, okay? Some men have it so good at home and are not even satisfied with a wife who cooks and cleans. She can bring home the bacon and fry it in a pan and bro' man still don't care.

And the bad part about all of this is you can't be mad at anybody because the structure of a family was not taught to us when we were growing up. In fact, in my family it was unnatural to us to see both mother and father in the same house. Now if you were to say step-mom and step dads or even new uncles this was normal to us. I think out of our whole family I only know of one aunt and uncle who were married and raising their own child. But if you were to listen to my mama she would tell you that something was wrong with them.

We must seek what the will of God is for our life. Out of all the wrong learning that has been instilled in my life at such a young age, I use to think of myself as damaged goods. It took me many years to unlearn and unload the garbage that was stunting my growth and my way of thinking towards people and towards me. I have family members that even today still confuse me with being that old damaged goods.

They will call and unload hateful and straight nasty talk about other family members and even some people that they don't even know.

I don't know if you can follow me when I tell you this but in order for me to find what God's will was for my life I had to lose my life. Now I know that you may be saying how do you lose your life without dying? And all I can tell you is that I did. I gave my all and all to God.

See, that way it would no longer be my life, but now it's God's life. And now I seek God's will and not my will. I have not perfected this way of life as of yet but I can tell you this much, I try to love always and to never let anyone take me out of this way. I try not to hear the bad news about my fellow brothers and sisters but to look for the good news about them. And I try to hear what you are saying to me and not see what you are doing instead.

And if you tell me that you love me but you don't love my mother, my father, my husband, my child, my sister or brother, not just my blood family but my new birth family as well, then I don't believe that the love of the father is in you. So, do you see why I must say that you know how to love me.

Owe no man anything, but to love one another:
for he that loved another hath fulfilled the law
Romans 13:8

*Though he slay me, yet will I trust
in him; but I will maintain mine
own ways before him.*
Job 13:15

*Owe no man anything, but to love
one another: for he that loveth
another hath fulfilled the law.*
Romans 13:8

CHAPTER 4

She Didn't Make Me, But She Did Try to Break Me

Before I started to write this chapter I prayed and fasted and even did a little soul searching. At one point I even started not to write this because it hurt so much just to remember all that took place. Putting this down on paper caused a light to shine in a dark place in my life. For me to do this now opens a door so that others may come in. Maybe now this place can heal and I can grow from the pain and release it.

For now I don't need a hiding place in my past to redeem myself as a person of today, and for all the times that I was told that I was nothing and would never become anything you were and are now wrong. I may not call names but my soul is a lot lighter now that I don't have to carry around your garbage any longer.

I can only ask what kind of adult finds pleasure in belittling and abusing a helpless child. At the age of two this person started to call herself my mother. I don't know how or why this was done to me but as I reached my early twenty's other family members started to tell bits and pieces of what they remembered or what was told to them. Since my father died he was not able to tell his side of the story. Being at the age that I was when I was taken from other family members the only thing that I have to go by is what others tell me. My relatives on my father's side tell me one story and my relatives on my mother's side tell me something else.

My step-mom has never told her side of the story. She only wants to be thought of as a hero or something because she kept someone's bastard child alive. At first I didn't want to see her or to hear her part in how she ended up with me. Now as the years go by and as God has dealt with me now I really do feel sorry for her because I don't know what my father told her. And I do know now that she went out of her way for me not to know that she wasn't really any kin to me. She changed my birth date and my age and even changed my name.

The part that I don't understand is that she had children of her own, so as a mother would she want someone to do her kids like she did me. One of her most famous sayings was that she would die and go to hell for her kids, but what I didn't know was that it meant everybody but me.

As I sit here this moment I can see me as the little scared kid trying to have someone to call mine, looking for someone to look to for guidance and affection, wanting someone to look down and see me and all that I could be in life. I can see me searching and searching but never finding this person. No matter where I looked in life this person could not be found.

Please, if you are blessed to be a part in a child's life no matter for how long, please do your part by helping to shape his future. If you put negative things into them, that is what you will get back. If you put positive and good into them this too, is what you will get.

You will be surprised at how you will be remembered in a younger person's life. We need to stop crying about how bad other folks children are, and how well mannered our kids are. Just look at your kids from someone else's point of view. They could be saying the same thing about your kids that you are saying about their kids.

If somebody came and told my step mother that we talked back to a grown-up she would curse you out because to have her tell it her children don't talk back to any grown up, when the truth of the matter is that if you were to run into any of her kids you would think of them as being very conceited and maybe even having a foul mouth.

From as far back as I can remember, you would never have heard my step mother ever say the words "love" or "I'm sorry" or "please" or "thank you." This is the big one; she would never say, "I was wrong." No, she would rather stop speaking, look you straight in the face and not speak.

Can you imagine living your whole young life never having anyone to hug and kiss you? The only physical contact that you ever received from her would be a whipping where she would grab you by one arm and start swinging whatever was in her other hand and that could be a leather belt or a switch or an inner tube off a bicycle or a broom handle.

Trust me when I tell you anything she got her hands on was her weapon for a whipping. It didn't matter much to her if she found nothing to hit you with cause she would back hand you or just straight out slap you. She has even been known to punch you and pull your hair. She didn't care. Hey, a broken tooth, a busted lip, a black eye, cracked ribs, those were her specialties.

After some time had gone by she would have the audacity to call you (when I say you it means me) over to her and look you over to see what damages she had done. If you were messed up pretty bad she would put some alcohol and other medicines on the wounds all the while saying "You brought this on yourself because you know how mad I can get" or "I don't know why you love to get me mad like that." Her favorite was "Do you see what you made me do; you must love to get whippings or something?"

Whether you were wrong or not she didn't care and if by some way she found out that she had beaten the wrong kid all she would say is "Well, you just got a whipping for something else that I don't know about." She never said, "I'm sorry," or let me take you to the local hospital or nothing. I believe that woman even put stitches in when the wounds were too deep.

I have a scar over one of my eyes from being pushed under a trailer with tin bent out and no doctor ever looked at it. Now that I think about it I don't remember being pushed under any trailer. That is what she told anyone who asked about the scar. Man, anything could have happened and to think I have been going around telling this same lie. Isn't that messed up?

One summer when some relatives come over to our house, all the children were allowed to play outside in the yard. The adults were in the front room talking about grown-up stuff and we were not allowed to go in the house for anything. If we needed something to drink we had to turn on the outside facet and drink water from there, and if you had to go pee then you had to find a bush or something. And God forbid if you had to do number two. You had to wait until the grown-ups stopped talking and ask permission to use the bathroom. If they thought that you were trying to listen to grown folks talk, they would say, "Go on and don't flush that toilet 'cause I need to see if you really had to go or if you just tryin' to be nosy."

Living with this woman was a living hell. You were not allowed to speak to any grown person and tell them anything and for God's sake don't let nobody ask you about a scar, broken tooth or something of that nature. If you answered, you were in trouble and if you didn't answer you were in trouble.

I remember one time a neighbor of ours said to my step-mom that out of all of her children I would be the one that she would love to have because I was the quietest and it seemed as though I was always off somewhere by myself. She never saw anyone ask me more than once to do anything. My step-mom said to her, "You are a big fool if you believe what you just said. Don't let that big-eyed black thing fool you."

Yep, she called me a "thing". She didn't think enough of me to call me by name, just called me "that thing."

Even though I wasn't old enough to know how little she thought of me, I still felt hurt and shame and belittled. She told the woman that she could do something with all of her kids but as for me that was a different story all together. For some reason she didn't care for me and she was going to do her best to make sure that nobody else would either.

If someone complimented me for any reason my step-mom would go nuts. One day one of my aunts said that I had a good grade of hair and that she wanted to start doing it for my mom. She cursed my aunt, her sister, out and told her to stop trying to make me feel like I was all that. Now if she wanted to spend some time with the other children then do so but don't come in her house trying to get anything started.

I really did like being around my aunt; she always had something nice for me and she never raised her voice. All she had to do is say, "Would you please do something for me?" and we would run over each other to do what she wanted. All the children loved her and loved to be around her, and for her to be my step-mom's sister was like day and night. The two of them were so different.

Now today I often look back over my life and I see what Mahalia Jackson was singing about when she sang, "How I Got Over" and yes, my soul does look back and wonder how I got over. I do believe that it was nothing that I did. It has only been by the grace of God for it has taken me a lot of years to come to the realization that I am not my own but I do belong to Jesus. I have been bought with price of his redeeming blood. Some people don't like it when saved souls speak of the blood but that's all I have. So all I can give is the Word of God.

The Lord is my light and my salvation; whom shall I fear? The Lord is the strength of my life; of whom shall I be afraid? When the wicked, even mine enemies and my foes, came upon me to eat up my flesh, they stumble and fell. Though an host should encamp against me, my heart shall not fear: though war should rise against me, in this will I be confident.

Psalm 27:1-3

*But they that wait upon the Lord
shall renew their strength; they
shall mount up with wings as
eagles; they shall run, and not be
weary; and they shall
walk, and not faint.*
Isaiah 40:31

CHAPTER 5

No One's Safe Any More

I know that about every other autobiography that you read that whether male or female, about seven out of ten of them have been sexually molested. It often becomes a way for the writer to give a voice to, or maybe to narrate their part in what happened. Years ago people just didn't talk about it, even though it appeared to be happening in everyone's family. No one ever thought hey, maybe we should take some sort of steps to protect our children from this senseless abuse. More than half of this type of abuse comes from a family member rather than a stranger.

From reading and doing research all the way back to biblical days there was some sort of sexual abuse of one family member raping other family members. When time permits read second Samuel the thirteenth chapter, where King David's son Amnon rapes his step-sister Tamar. When a person is raped, from that moment nothing in life will ever be the same again. I don't care how hard a person tries to forget, you never will forget this act of violence that has been done to you and when you try to look at it from the abuser's view point I can't for the life of me understand how any grown up can look at any child and have sexual feeling towards them. It sickens me to my stomach whenever I hear a sexual offender say that he could not help himself.

I would like for someone to explain how a person can look at a baby or a young child and find them to be sexually attractive? With every fiber of my being I can't understand it, and I do really believe that person to be self-centered, narcissistic, unfeeling, and just uncaring.

Think about the innocent and helpless babies and younger children who haven't done anything to anyone; they only know one thing and that is to love. They need protection from anyone who can't see them for being the blessing that they are.

I am only giving my opinion and I know that someone may think completely differently about this. Some of you may be saying the person you are talking about is your family member. All I can say to you is this person is my family member, too.

This thing has gotten to be so big in our environment that if you were in a large crowd of people and you were to count every fourth person this person could be a sex offender. And if you have been sexually abused I don't want you to forget, but I do want you to forgive because if you don't forget you will be able to help someone else who has been going through, or you may see the signs and be able to prevent it from happening to someone else.

And just maybe we can get together and find a way to stop this senseless crime against our children and their children. And when I ask that you forgive them this will lighten your walk as you travel down your path in life; you will not stumble and fall because there is no longer a stumbling block there. And even though you have forgiven your offender, they have no power over you. Stand up and take your life back.

Now I don't want you to just believe that everyday people are hurting our children. We have some church folks doing some ungodly things to children and hiding behind the cross. However, I am here to let them know that I don't care what you do in the dark, oh, it will come to light and the cross is not covering your shameful sins. And even though some years may have passed by it's not over. Some way, somehow, it will come right back to you. There have been times when those people are exposed that others try to cover up what they have done by sending them away to other churches. Instead of the person ceasing their wrong doings, they look at it as an opportunity to start anew.

We wonder why some people have such a hard time coming to church and seeking Christ for leadership and guidance in their life. We often say they are not ready to surrender everything to God, when all the while not knowing that this person has had an extremely bad experience with the church.

A lot of the time we misinterpret what is going on. Not everybody is ready to talk about what happened to them. It sometimes takes people a life time to open up and expose their attacker. And if this person is you or you know of a person like this don't take their hesitation as an excuse to not wanting to be bothered. Sometimes when some one else comes out and exposes their offender it encourages other victims to come forward and tell their stories.

I have seen some cases where the priest or pastors who are accused of molestation are not excommunicated, but are just sent to another location to start over again. I believe this has hindered a lot of families from seeking the church and its help.

And now we can't even send our little ones off to nursery or child care without worrying if someone is going to touch them inappropriately. This has become such a problem that even the baby sitter's back ground must be researched. Folks are getting paid for teaching you how to spy on the nannies and other child care people. I remember when I was younger and in school and even before grade school if someone in the house was over the age of ten that's all you needed. They were your baby-sitter and you ate whatever they could fix for you to eat. And we had to do what we were told to do and not only that, we had to clean the house up from top to bottom. We washed and cleaned windows, dishes, and clothes. And when my step-mom would leave she didn't worry about what we were doing; she would go and do whatever it was that she did and for as long as she wanted to.

Now I know that you may be saying that's not a good thing, but I promise you that if something happened when my step-mom did come home all she had to do was to say: "What happened while I was gone?" And everyone would start telling on each other and before you knew it everybody would be getting a whipping, so the next time she was gone everyone would be spying on each other trying to get the goods on each other. And when it was school time all my step-mom would do is find a family member or a neighbor who didn't work and she would come to some sort of agreement and that was that.

I remember my step-mom got one of her sisters who had a nervous condition to watch us. A couple of times she lost it for whatever reason and had to go to a mental hospital. To compound the problem, she also drank a lot of beer. When she would come over to watch us we had to go outside and stay out of her way. She would watch her stories, drink her beer and talk to the television. She would eat raw onions and sardines, and feed us kids mayonnaise sandwich and give us sugar water to drink.

When my step-mom came home, we would tell on her. My step-mom would say to us is: "You ate, didn't you? So hush and mind your business." We tried to tell her that our aunt brought someone over and fed him all the lunch meat. She didn't care that we could have gotten a sun stroke from being outside in the sun all day. If we came in the house my aunt would make us get in bed and stay there.

And this one time we tried to tell our mom that her sister was having her boy friend come over to our house and that they were doing the nasty in the house all the while we had to be outside. My step-mom didn't care.

"Stop trying to be grown. Stay in a child's place," she would say to us.

But one day my step-mom came home early. We all came running in the house behind her because we knew that something was about to go down and sure enough it did.

My step-mom was fussing at her sister, the same one who was supposed to have the mental problem.

"What in the hell is going on in here and what are your drawers doing on my kitchen table"?

"They are minding their own damn business and why don't you try to do the same damn thing, okay!"

All of us children hollered and started to laugh. I promise you, I don't believe that I will ever forget that day.

And when I tell you this, my step-mom didn't care who she got to watch her kids. I remember this one blind lady that she got to watch my little brother because all of us older kids had to go to school. Now for the life of me I still can't figure out how this blind woman could change a baby's diaper.

Now that I think about it, I believe the blind lady drank beer too. Now how did she baby sit someone's kid blind and drunk? I remember some times when we picked up our little brother, his clothes would be on the wrong side, you know, inside out. And sometimes the little fellow would have on a little girl's shirt. At first, we thought that maybe he had missed up his clothes, only to find out that she thought they were his clothes. It is no wonder that so many of us turned out to be dysfunctional.

But to go back to what I was saying nowadays you can't hardly trust anyone with your kids any more. You look on the news or in a newspaper only to find out that some ones daycare center had to be closed because someone has touched a little kid and now the little kid is asked to show what happened to them. Each day, parents must question their kids as a safeguard and ask, "What did you do in school today, Billy?"

And we have to teach our little ones to come and let us know if somebody touches them on their private parts. It is difficult for a kid nowadays to be at peace and learn anything if they have to constantly watch and be on guard for everything. They can't even play blocks and clay dough with the other kids. I really don't know what this world is coming to. We as a society have to do better when it comes to our little ones.

Now I don't want to leave anyone out. We have those who are supposed to be teaching our kids but some of those guys are looking at the children as available dates and a quick "bootie call" or new "meat" or something. When a parent sends their kids to school they want to have peace of mind and not have to be bothered with the prospect of who is out there sizing up their child to exploit and take advantage of them.

These days we give kids too much freedom. We don't talk to them or ask them about their day. It's like some of us are saying I won't ask you anything and don't you tell me anything. I have heard some folks say that they don't know what their child wore to school, and some of them can't even tell you the location of their child's bus stop.

Some of the cases where the teachers are fooling around with the kids, months have gone by and the parent doesn't even hear about it firsthand. Someone tells them about it. Most of the time, the abuse has been going on so long that the kid thinks that he is in a relationship or going steady with the teacher. And almost all of these teachers go home to a spouse and children of their own.

Some of our young girls are even becoming pregnant from teachers, and in some cases the female teacher has gotten pregnant from male students. Now what I want to know is just what kind of relationship is an adolescent suppose to have with an adult? I mean don't the teachers have to be sensible and have some sort of consideration for our kids? First of all, what kind of job can this young immature inexperienced child get, and who is expected to buy diapers and everything else that a baby needs. Who is going to support who?

I can't feel sympathetic for any adult who sits around contemplating any kind of sexual act towards a child. I don't care how mature they look for their age, I can't emphasize this enough as a parent, an aunt and even a grandmother. We need to make ourselves available for our children to communicate with us, and not the other way around. It is our jobs to protect all the children, not just our own.

We have got to start right now, today. I know that some of you may be saying how can I make a difference? We must start speaking out in our community whenever we see our young boys walking around with their pants hanging down off their butts. We need to let them know that it does not look good, and if you as an adult believe that it does look good, then guess what, you may be one of the very persons that we are trying to protect them from.

And when we see our young girls dressing to show more skin then clothes we need to teach them what it means to cover up. Not everybody should be having conversations on how to dress our young adults because how can you teach anyone anything if you haven't been taught?

When we don't do our part and say something when we see it, we become part of the problems rather than the solution. We as a society seem to feel better standing behind closed doors and making accusations about other folks and how they are raising their children. We ask ourselves what's wrong with the world today. But I am saying that if you know what's wrong then why don't you open your door and speak up! I am not going to push the blame on no one else. I can only say what I know I have done. I use to see something and would turn my head the other way. I remember one time telling a close friend of mine that I started to say something but the kid might say something back, or how I did say something and how grown the kid was by cursing and being rude. And for the life of me I don't know when it happened but all of a sudden I became sensitive.

I don't want any of you to think that I believe that the problem is someone else's responsibility for what is going on with our kids today. We all tend to point our fingers at the next person. We say that it comes from the rap music and movies that are being made, but I have been told that whenever you point a finger at someone else that there is always three fingers pointing back at you.

We need to start investing in our young people and that doesn't always mean money; you can make a difference by spending some time with our youth. Just do something positive. And we must love our children in words and in deeds.

Let's start telling our children how beautiful they are. Let's show them affection at home so that when somebody in the streets and in schools or wherever they may go tell them something like this, that it will not go to their heads and when it is said to them a red flag goes up and tells them to leave at once.

I believe that a lot of our youth are following behind these molesters and not being over powered. These people know just what our young boys and girls little ears are itching to hear. We need to validate them as being the treasures that they are. They need to know when they are in harm's way. You know, like when you are in the company of a rattle-snake to run and not stay because you like the sound of the rattle. It is a tragedy for our children to not be able to protect themselves from the very people who have taken as oaths to teach and guide them into becoming a greater society.

Gandhi once said "Be the changes that you want to see in the world." So as for me and my household we are going to become doers of what needs to be done, and not just talkers of what's wrong with everybody and everything. I don't believe that the kids of today want to be talked at but they would much rather be spoken to with the same love and respect as every human being does Someone once said "You must pick one, either you live for yesterday or you can start to live for tomorrow,but you have to pick one."

So let's get involved with our future.

Lo, children are an heritage of the Lord: and the fruit of the womb is his reward.
Psalm 127:3

Ask of me, and I shall give thee the heathen for thine inheritance, and the uttermost parts of the earth for thy possession.

Psalm 2:8

CHAPTER 6

No, I Didn't Ask for This

I remember coming up as a kid some years ago. When ever something went wrong or I got hurt, I almost never failed to hear these words from my step-mom.

"You asked for it to happen, now shut up."

How does a person ask to get hurt?

I remember on one occasion when I was in gym class and we were playing dodge ball and I jumped in the air to catch the ball, my finger got jammed somehow and my hand swole up. When I got home I showed it to my step-mom and tried to explain to her how it had happened.

"Don't come crying to me. You had to have been doing something that you had no business doing cause people's fingers just don't get jammed from catching a ball. You are always doing something and getting yourself hurt and when you get hurt you want everyone and their mama's mom to come running to help you. You ask for it to happen so now you must suffer the consequences."

And here is another thing that she liked to say whenever someone got hurt:

"You are old enough to know better; what's wrong with you? You must be a pain freak. Do you like hurting yourself or are you just stupid, because even a blind person with half of a brain would know better than to do the stupid things that you do. You are so clumsy you may as well have two left feet. It is a wonder you even have any blood left to bleed out. I wouldn't be surprised if dust just came out of your veins, so don't come crying to me when you get hurt because I am going to whip you. I tell you all the time to stop doing dumb things. Out of all people, you should know how clumsy you are and you are always getting hurt."

She of all people shouldn't be saying this to me because over half of the injuries that I got was because of her. She would ask me about something and if my answer was not what she wanted she would backhand me out of nowhere and afterwards she would say "I didn't want to hit you but you made me do it." And then she would finish it off with "Now get out of my sight before I give you something to cry about." What was wrong with this picture as if being hurt wasn't enough to cry for, dumb I know. I truly do believe that if someone would say to me have a seat and start writing down all the crazy stuff that was said to you from child hood until now I would be able write a book the size of a phone book.

I use to believe that my step-mom came up with all of those sayings. She might not have come up with them all but I can guarantee you that she got her share of them in. I do believe that she could very well be the author for coming up with the dumbest sayings.

And for God's sake don't ever come to her bleeding because her answer for it would be to pour some green alcohol on it. If you needed stitches or half you hand was hanging off, she would come out of nowhere with a bottle of rubbing alcohol as if she was waiting for something to happen. Sometime I would be crying more because of the alcohol burning than because of the actual injuries.

That woman was a piece of work. If you fainted from the shock of the stinging alcohol on a gaping wound she would use the same green alcohol and put it under your noise to revive you. And if you were lucky enough to make it to the hospital the first thing they would ask why pressure was not applied to the wound to stop the bleeding. Do you know that she would stand right there in front of those medically trained doctors and nurses and tell them that they didn't know the first thing about fixing people. Oh, she would carry on like they were lucky that she was there to teach them a thing or two. She would say things like "How on earth did they get a good paying job like this at a hospital and not know nothing," or "Someone must be related to someone else or know someone in a high places to have gotten this job."

I would sit there not knowing whether to be sick or just shamed-faced but I did know one thing; whatever I did for God's sake I had better not pull a fainting number because she would have that green rubbing alcohol under my noise in no time at all. And for the longest I didn't know that every time a person came to the hospital they keep records of everyone by social security number and first and last names.

So my step-mom had six children and this meant that she showed up quite often or in their case more than the doctors and medical staff wanted to see her. Have you ever heard of a jail house lawyer, well, my step-mom was a back woods self proclaimed midwife only she wasn't trained for anything nor was she anybody's wife. Now the medical staff knew that whenever she was there that she came along with all kinds of drama. There is no telling what those people wrote in our files.

Now that I am able to look back on my past, there were many childhood injures. I know that every child will get hurt in some kind of way so I don't feel so bad now as I look on my past. And through it all I have learned what the word past means, meaning it has already happened; either I must live in yesterday or live for tomorrow.

When I look at the news on TV or read the newspaper, I usually try not to think anything bad about anyone especially whoever it is that hurt people for no good reasons. When I say for no good reasons I mean that it is not done in self defense or you are not protecting someone. Now when someone just goes around hurting and killing people I kind of have a problem with this and I do all that I can do for me not to dislike people, because I believe that I can pretty much get along with anyone. I do have a problem with not liking some of the things that people do. But I struggle with it only because the Bible tells me that I must love everyone. God has done a wonderful heart transplant within me and I don't want to go backwards in my spiritual walk with my Lord and Savior.

Do you know that if you pay too much attention to what is going on in the news, you can fall into a sinful state of mind? I know you are wondering how. I don't know about you but I start acting like I am a judge and depending on how bad the crime may be I have a tendency to want something just as bad to happen to the criminals. You know, like in the Old Testament–an eye for an eye and a life for a life--and so on. So sometime I have to stop and ask myself what would Jesus do? And before I know it I get my answer. Yes, what would he do and guess what, I am not Jesus and I don't have a heaven nor hell to place anyone in.

There have been times when I had to stop trying to put myself above others by judging them. Now I just do the right thing and pray for others. I have learned to let God do his job and do his will for me and that is to love and to pray for others.

I sometimes tend to get into trouble when praying for others because I tend to over think everything and my heart won't allow me to forgive people as I should. So when I find myself in this situation, I say. "Lord you know everything, not only what is going on with others, but Lord you know me as well; so I ask you to forgive everyone including me."

I tend to have problems when someone says that the reason why they did what they did was because they were abused as a child. Well, who wasn't? Then someone says, "Oh, I did it because I have a mental problem that makes me go around hurting and killing people." My thoughts on this is why didn't you start on your killing spree with yourself first? Why should everyone else suffer because you are sick, and why not take the parents along to jail with them for turning someone unstable on society without any warning.

You know what I am saying, like give everyone else the opportunity to be on guard so that they (the world) can protect themselves and their family members. I believe that a lot of the violence that has been committed could have been avoided. All it would have taken is for someone to come forth and say. "Hey, this person is an unsafe person and someone needs to keep an eye on them." But we don't want to get into other folk's business but God forbid that the roles were the other way around. We would want a person to go that extra mile of knocking on our door and alerting us.

I remember hearing about a young lady who was raped and killed. The perpetrator set her remains on fire to conceal evidence. That was the sickest think I had ever heard of because this was done to someone's child. Now add to this the criminal wants to act as if everything is back to normal, like nothing has happened so that this person can sit back to see if it was all out of their system.

All the while the media is giving all the information that they can, not about the criminal, but about the victim. With the information that is given we get a small glimpse of what this person did, but not who this person was. I can remember hearing someone say that the way she dressed, she must have been asking for something like that to happen to her. Someone even asked why was she out there at that time of night anyhow. All I could say is what does that have to do with anything. What kind of out-fit says, "Hey, come and rape me. Look, I have on my 'come kill me' shoes and look at this, here is my 'set my body on fire' pocket book to go along with it." When I hear this it causes me to wonder what if this was a family member of the person who says this stuff. How would you feel hearing a statement so negative coming from the community that you live in. You would think that the death of anyone should require respect and even a moment of silence.

How can it be that our hearts have become so hard and so cold; our feelings have become so dull and dark. And this is much too critical for the human race. It is like we are moving in the wrong direction in life.

One day at church prior to dismissal, the Bishop told a story about an incident reported in the news. A young man was bitten by a shark. I thought the Bishop was going to say, "Let's pray for this young man." Instead, he said the young man got what he deserved because he was out there where the shark lived and the shark did what sharks do. Now I told this story for a reason and that is to say that this world as we know it is filled with so much hypocrisy and double standards. We have become so inconsiderate of others people's situations.

And here is this bishop who is supposed to be sensitive and sympathetic to other's needs, so who are we supposed to go to for consolation in our times of grief? The religious folks are taking all the good out of God's words and showing inconsistencies with the saved folks that really do care about doing what the Bible tells us to do and the needs of others. You know we really do need to be our brother's keeper.

This same bishop spoke harshly about a television pastor who had accusations made against him. Whatever he had done made him and his family look bad; his behavior made the church look bad. Not just this church, but all churches were slandered because of this one pastor. Now because of this individual's action anyone who went to church was looked at differently.

The bishop that discussed this matter was tearing this other pastor apart. He had absolutely no regards whatsoever for this man of God who had fallen. There were no kind words for his family nor were there feelings of sorrow for this pastor's church members. And this bishop never once said, "Let's see if this guy is innocent of what he is being accused of doing."

All I am saying is if the church is treating other church members this way what can we expect from the rest of the world? I pray that a change will happen soon because the way that things are going nowadays, if people don't know God for themselves and pray for themselves, we as a people will have nowhere to run to for help. And if we do go to church for help must of the time the only thing that they

want to know is what church are you a member of
and please don't tell them that you are not a member
because they are going to tell you that this is why
you are having all the problems. In other words, you
asked for this to happen to you.

But hey, what about the church folks and their
problems? Guess what, they even have something
for you too, where is your faith? Yes, oh you of little
faith, you need to go on a fast and pray for your
answer. If you don't get an answer then it must not
be meant for you to have whatever it is that you are
seeking for. O.k. now I don't want you to think that
I don't believe in the church or in the power of
prayer because I truly do believe in it and I'm not
saying that all churches are alike.

There is this other bishop that I know and this
guy really knows his gift of being able to study the
Bible and then break it down and teach it so that
even a kid could understand it. I called on him when
I had loaned some money to a person in need and I
know how I am about this kind of thing. It's like
seven out of ten times when money is involved I fall
out of friendship with the person that has borrowed
it from me.

I wanted to be wise about lending this money so
I prayed and ask God what I should do. I received an
answer on the matter which was, do not lend it if I
could not afford to lose it. But me being me, I did it
anyways and from the moment on our relationship
changed. I like to call her my sister in Christ.
Whenever she would laugh your spiritual being
could feel the depths of her sincerity. After the
money changed hands all of that was gone. From

then on whenever our paths crossed, it became tremendously difficult to even talk and now her laugh seems to be hollow and empty.

Now I need for bishop to get right to the point and apply the word to my situation. So I called him and I was feeling sorry for myself because I knew better about what I had done. Not only did I not have the money. Now I also didn't have this sister in Christ any more. So when I did get to share my trouble with bishop he didn't let me down. He prayed and I cried. He didn't just pray and say, "OK, good-bye." He gave me such good insight on what I had done. He told me that my heart was in a good place but my brains were in a bad place. I can't help everybody; sometimes I need to be able to just be there to listen and to pray with people who are having financial trouble. It does not mean that I have to lend money. He also told me that there are other ways to be there for people like finding programs through the community that gave assistance and other grants to help people when they are in need. If they were not able to help then sometimes they could refer us to someone who could help.

You know now whenever someone calls me and say that they need my help I try to not over extend myself in any way. I found that it is less stressful and I don't have to fall out with anyone.

Sometimes I sit back and reflect on how wonderful it would be if I could bless others as I have been blessed. I want to do something for a family who is in need or to be able to give hope to an individual. I don't want to do something nice to be able to talk about it or show off what I can do. I want to do something nice because I am asked.

Sometimes the compassion within me wishes that I could do something for every needy family, like pay a bill for them so that it would be one less head ache and just maybe someone will be able to get a good night's rest without the stress and worries of the things that we can't control in life.

I remember one time someone came to me and asked for some help because there was nowhere else for her to go. All I could do was worry about what kind of a person am I to not be able to help her, So instead of trying to find another way to get her help for what she needed, I gave what I had which was not enough to get her out of the trouble that she was in but just enough to buy her some time and be able to get a decent nights rest. And because I didn't think about my own troubles, I now needed a loan to get me out of this mess. And all I could think of was that I asked for this to happen because I knew that I could not afford to lend any amount of money out because every dollar that I had was already accounted for to pay bills. Now here I am not able to sleep at night for worrying, doing as the old folks use to say "trying to rob Peter to pay Paul program."

I don't know that I would change anything if I had it to do over because my strength in serving Christ is making sacrifices for others I don't want to be one of those church goers who do good things for people because I believe that in return God will bless me for doing good. I want to be one of those God fearing church folks who do helpful things for people because it is the right thing to do and in the end I don't believe that when a person does what is right they should be rewarded for it. And if it means that I must suffer for the cause then so be it so maybe I did ask for it, because I do remember in a prayer asking God to allow me to become a lender and not a borrower, and to be the head and not the tail.

You know there are times when I can't comprehend some of the things that God puts on my mind and a lot of times things don't make any sense. Sometimes this small voice within me says to give away what I have set aside for my family's needs such as utilities and other things that money is needed for. The funny thing is the money that is being set aside is most often not enough to pay all of the bills in full any ways.

But here is the point that I am trying to emphasize. My utilities have never been disconnected and our household has not gone without. Anytime I have been led to give what I have to help someone else and I am not obedient it never fails a bill collector shows up at the door looking for some money.

As I pray days and nights, my supplication to God is for his will to be done in my life and for me to be a blessing to others. I do not want to be a hindrance to anyone. Sometimes I get the feeling that everything I have prayed for is being fulfilled. I don't know if I can explain the feeling that comes with it, the stillness and warm peaceful sensation of God's presence. All that I can hear in my spirit is ask and believe. Some nights I don't sleep at all. I make a list in my mind of all the work that needs to be done and how little time and money I have.

I am a believer that God will not give me a vision without a way to bring it to pass. I sometimes get discouraged while I am waiting for my break-though because I am eager to start helping a larger amount of God's people. With all that is going on in this day and time, I believe that there is a need in every household. Every now and then the Lord sends a word of confirmation to let me know to just hold on.

No, I didn't ask for any of this to happen in my life, but I do deserve what is being done in my life. And when I die I don't want to be remembered as the person who had an unfulfilled dream. Let me say this first and foremost, there is absolutely nothing wrong with having a dream. Without a dream, there would be no vision. I want to be known as the person who did the work that was needed to be done to bring a dream to life.

For everything that has been written here in this chapter I pray that it will be a blessing to you; and to God be the glory.

He giveth power to the faint; and to them that have no might he increaseth strength. Even the youths shall faint and be weary, and the young men shall utterly fall; but they that wait upon the Lord shall renew their strength; they shall mount up with wings as eagles; they shall run, and not be weary; and they shall walk, and not faint.
Isaiah 40:29-31

Is this house, which is called by my name, become a den of robbers in your eyes? Behold, even I have seen it, saith the Lord.

Jeremiah 7:11

CHAPTER 7

Is Mama Going to Pick Him Over Me?

B y now you may have figured out that I never had a good relationship with any adult in my family as I was growing up. So this meant that there was no one that I could go to that I could tell about all of the horrible things that were being done to me. Nor could I share any of the life changing events that I survived.

Out of all the abuse that I had been through from my step-mom and other folks I never knew that my real mother was about a twenty-four bus ride away from where I was. I wonder how long she looked for me after my father took me from my real family members. I was taken from a place they call the north where it is very cold.

My family didn't have a relationship where the kid's well-being or happiness came ahead of the adult's friendships. If my step-mom wanted to have sexual relations with some guy, it didn't matter what the kids thought of him. A lot of times we would have never seen this person before. All we were told is "This here is your new uncle and that's that." I use to wonder how a mother could pick a man over her child. Most of the time when the man came into the picture he left behind his own kids for some other guy to come in and to do the same thing that he is doing in this family.

Being in the situation that I was in of not being the oldest nor the youngest or for that matter not even being born into this family, the odds were already against me for my step-mom's new man friend to like me. Back in those days the new boy friend was call our new "uncle." I don't understand how my mom could bring some strange fellow into a house with little girls living there, because who's to say that this new uncle wouldn't try anything with us.

We already had to be on guard with our old uncles and now here she comes with a new uncle. For all we knew about our new uncles he could have been some mad man who could have just killed his old family or something. Now I don't know why she would tell us this because as a young kid just trying to understand the logic of having your mother and her brother or your dad's brother sleeping in the same room and to be doing some of the things that they were doing, I thought this must be a special uncle or this was just a crazy family.

This new uncle would give my step-mom money and tell her to send us to the store or somewhere to get us out of the house so that they could be alone. Now this was new for us because we were not allowed to be outside after it had gotten dark, but now we could be outside on a school night. So now nothing mattered to our mom but to keep our new uncle happy. Nothing good could come from this because I could not get over how much in love she was with this guy that she just met and she was even crazier for his money.

All I knew was I would never do the things that she was doing with this so called new uncle. Besides, whose brother was he any way. The first chance that I got I was going to find out how was he our uncle. For this very reason I stayed in trouble, because a person couldn't just tell me anything and it was over because if it didn't set well with my soul I would not receive it well. Every since I can remember myself I would make a face, I don't just hear something and think about it, somehow it always shows on my face that something is wrong with this picture. I knew I would not be doing the stuff that she was doing with any brother of mine. I can't emphasize on how many levels of sickness that this was for me.

Now if I was confused at the age that I was, what about the other kids that were younger than me. And when the new uncle would start coming around, some of their behavior was manipulative to us young girls. He would say things like "when you all grow up you will have all kinds of men falling at your feet, both young and old and you all don't need to get married because you can have a man for everyday of the week and they will be happy to give you all their hard earned money." He would tell us to have a man for every bill that needed to be paid, and if they didn't want to pay our bills just send them stepping.

One time we saw him out in the streets with a group of other men so we went over to where he was. We spoke to him but he didn't answer us so we went a little closer so that he could see and hear us better. He kept turning his head as if he was looking over our heads, so we call him 'uncle' and the other men folk that were with him started to laugh and holler at him and he say to some other guy that was out there "Hey, last week you were the new uncle" and to another guy that last month he was playing uncle.

We know that this meant something bad, so when we reached home we told our mom what had happened and we just knew that this cat would be long gone whenever our mom would see him again, only to find out that she ended up making us apologize to him. She made us say that we were wrong for trying to make him look bad in front of his friends. She said that because of what we had done now everyone in town would know her business and that she should beat all of us because she raised us to stay out of grown folks faces.

I couldn't believe that she had the audacity to fall for whatever it was that he had said. It was as if our feelings didn't matter to her. And all was well with her and dear old uncle, but as for us, she could care less and she ended up telling us to stay out of grown folks faces and out of her business. She would say hateful things to us kids and one time she told me that I had a problem with staying in a child's place.

And on more than one occasion she said to me that it was all my fault that she was unhappy. I can remember this one time when she slapped me across

my face and said that she had to break up with this
guy that really did look out for her, and that he didn't
seem to mind that she had a lot of kids. This man
was someone that was right for her, and that he could
have helped her in many ways. But me and my no
good father seems to always find a way to get into
her business.

Most of the time, I didn't know what she was
talking about. I didn't understand how this was my
fault or how my father knew about this new uncle.
All I could think of was this uncle must not be my
father's brother after all. Whenever she got in this
type of mood I kind of knew to stay clear of her
because when she was hurt she wanted someone else
to be in pain too and that someone most always
turned out to be me.

Hurt people do hurtful things to other people.
Misery loves company. Whoever came up with those
sayings must have known my step-mom.

I can't be specific about the number of single
mothers that there are today, and I can't tell you how
far back in history that the term "single moms" came
about. To have knowledge of this may turn out to be
insufficient because not all mothers are the same
especially when the mother's love for her child is
genuine. No matter what happened, whether the kids
are at fault or the new guy does something wrong,
the love that the mother has for her child will and
should always come first. Even if this means that the
relationship between the mother and the new boy
friend has to come to an end then so be it. I am not
saying that the children get to run their mother's life
and that the mother can't have any kind of

relationship because the mother should be happy, and a good mother can make them both work.

Some mothers know how to separate their love life from their children's lives until Mister Right comes alone and they get married and become one big happy family. But then there are some mothers who don't love their kids. Yes, this is true that some mothers don't love their kids. There may be some who love their kids but don't love the things that their kids do.

I have heard of some women being raped and at a later time found out she was pregnant. The mother may decide to keep the child but in the end the child suffers because no matter how bad the mother may want it to work, the only thing that she sees when she looks at her child's face is an act of violence that was done to her; there was no love in the making of the child.

No matter how much she may want a loving relationship with her child, without some sort of counseling, it may become a generational curse. At some time later in the future the child may have kids of their own and because of the strained relationship that he or she had with their mother it could go over to their kids, and then the next set of parents and so on. But this mother could get married and have other children out of love and no matter how much she may want to love the first child the same as the love child, the pain will still be there. It will only keep getting worse as time goes on. She still may learn how to love this child, but it will only happen with work and prayer. Then maybe she can see that the child could not be at fault, but the child was a victim as well.

Now she finds herself caring more for the love child then the first child and believe it or not the children can tell the difference in the way that they are being treated. Even though no one has said anything to them about what is going on with their mother and their older sibling, they know that something has happened and can comprehend that mama's love for them is not the same.

I have heard it said before that a person can love you, but not like you or your ways. But how can this be? I mean the things that you do and say are who you are. And I have also heard from a kid's point of view that they feel as though their mom didn't love them as much as she loved her boy friend, or they felt as though they were the black sheep of the family. And this word I have found tends to come up more and more as I meet other families. To tell you the truth, I can't say for sure that I have ever seen a family who didn't have one.

Please don't misinterpret what I am saying. I am not saying that every family has a black sheep, I am just saying most families do and a lot of the time if you ask the mother about it she will tell you that she loves all of her children the same. In fact, she will probably be surprised to hear that one of her kids believes themselves to be black-sheep.

And there have been times when the children will have different fathers and one father treated the mother good and even though the father may not still be together with the mother he shows her respect and helps with his responsibility of raising their child.

And the other child's father might treat her bad and not help out with the kid. The mother may have had to degrade herself by running the father around town asking and pleading with him for some type of support only to hear him say that he is not her baby's daddy. She may find out that he's with some other woman and is taking care of some other guy's kids. I can just imagine how hurt the feelings would be for this single mother.

The shame of this may cause her to start having hurtful feelings toward her child, and every time she looks at his child she could still be feeling the hurt and shame. So now when this smooth talking Mr. Johnny-come-lately comes along, her only concern is what she must do to keep this man.

There are some mothers who have such a low self esteem that they start to settle for less in what they need in life from a man and the type of role models that she needs to be in her kid's life. I remember this one young lady said to me that she didn't feel whole without having a man in her bed at night, and I said to her that if it takes another person to make you whole then you need Jesus and not a man, because what if he doesn't feel whole then instead of there being two people now all you've got is two different half's that don't go together.

I said, that "Jesus is who you should be looking for because he will never leave you nor forsake you. And he will never cheat on you nor will he abuse you or your children and he will stick closer to you then a brother. He will be everything that you need in a man. He will go everywhere with you, not just in your bed. He don't mind being with you, and you don't have to let your standards down with him. He will teach you how to love yourself and your kids, and he will never ask you to chose to love him and not your children."

Everyone else that you come in contact with will want to run your household and everyone that lives with you. And I told her that if she just needed a man to go to bed with her then she will never be whole because she is asking for trouble. This man will not respect her nor will he ever take her serious. The two will never have a foundation to build on. She was setting herself up for failure just to be able to say that she has a man.

This guy may be sleeping with her but he sure enough won't be respecting her or her house-hold. This is not showing her little girls anything positive to look forward to in life, for having her family when she gets older, and it doesn't teach her little boys how to grow up and become Godly men.

Who will teach the children how to function in a relationship when the time comes for them to be the parents? This same single mother had six children, but she didn't have all of her kids living with her because some of the children's father had taken their children with them when they split, so she got a little break. One day she repeated something to me that was said to her by her "wannabe player" of a boy friend. I couldn't for the life of me believe that she had accepted this statement that he said to her "No man is going to want to be with any woman who has as many children as you do."

And he told her that she should be grateful that he was there and that he was doing what little that he was doing for her, and that she needed to keep her children away from him because if he had wanted somebody's kids in his face every time he turned around he would have stayed where his kids were at.

That alone would have been more than enough for me, but we all have different boiling points, I guess. So I asked her what did she do when he said this to her and she said that "Oh, he was just talking and I don't pay him no mind. He didn't mean anything. You know how folks run their mouth when they are drinking." I told her that a drunken mouth speaks a sober word, and that she was asking for trouble as long as this person was hanging around her and her kids. Now she has a child from him and he could care less if the kids have anything to eat or have a roof over their heads. Not only does he not try to help her with the other children but he won't do for his own child that he has with her.

She called me crying one night about how he had told her that he don't like her kids and that they were too grown for him and that she is going to have to beat them and teach them to stay out of her affairs or he will leave her, and that she will always be alone and unhappy with no man to love her. I asked her if she gave him a piece of her mind and then put him out of her house? All that she could said to me was "no." She said that every couple goes through something and that it would work out somehow.

Do you know that she had the nerve to quote one of Ms. Betty Wright's songs to me and say "You know having a piece of a man is better than having no man at all." So I told her that the guy that she was with is not even a piece of a man, and that at the beginning she was looking for a man, now she is settling for just a piece of a man. I told her that I really do believe that she fell and bumped her head.

I felt like she has already picked and put this guy before her kids, and that she already knew what she was going to do about him. So I didn't even waste my breath by asking her what was she going to do about her children and their well-being? But I did tell her that she needed to rethink the type of messages that she was sending her kids. I feel that her kids will see that they might not be first in her life after all. I don't think she believes that she could do better, so if she doesn't believe that she can do better what could I tell her?

She was not a bad looking person. Actually, she was a nice person who wanted more out of life, but didn't know how to go about making it happen for her and her kids. I don't think she could see what effect this mean spirited person was having on her and her kid's relationship with each other! She became so obsessed with this guy that she stopped taking care of her children's needs. She had in her mind that she had to have a man. When I think about how bad he treated her and her children, I don't know who to feel sorry for, her or the kids. I say her because she lost sight of everything, all of her dreams and plans that she had for her and her family.

Whenever I hear of a stepfather mistreating the children of his girl friend, my mind tends to go into overdrive. I have a list of things that I ask myself: 1) Where is the mother while this abuse is going on? 2) Where is the biological father? and does he know about his child being abused, and what is he going to do about it? 3) Where are the grand parents ? 4) Who is going to call the cops, and why haven't they already been called? 5) What about the children, what is being done to get the children to a safe place?

Whenever a child's well-being is being endangered and I find out about it, I don't stop until I know that something is being done about it. Whether the child is related to me or not I can't rest or have a moment of peace until I know that something is being done about it. I feel that someone has got to speak up for the children; they must come first. I really can't stand any type of abuse, but the children are the most helpless. They can't defend themselves as a grown up is able to do so. And they do not ask for a person to come into their lives and do harm to them, and they can't fight off a grown person like another grown up can.

So I am speaking to all you single mothers out there. I know that you need love too. But please don't ever let anyone tear you from giving your little ones 100% of your love for them Please don't ever make your child feel un-wanted and please always let them know that they can do all things through Christ Jesus who strengthen us.

Our children are our future. For all of you single mothers, if you have to have a new man in your life, please let him know from day one that in your house, the kids are always first. If he wants to be with you, he is going to have to step up to the plate and not only share in the responsibility of raising the children in your home but he needs to go back and do for his children as well. Don't allow anyone to mistreat them. Let them know that you are there for them and that you want what is best for them.

I ask that if you have gotten anything out of this chapter that you will invest into a child's life and I do pray that you have opened your eyes and your heart. Help someone today. It does not have to be anything big and you don't even have to let that person know that you have done something for them. I believe that a change will come, but it needs to start with one person. Will you be that one?

If I do a good deed for someone, and in return if I can ask of that person only one thing, then it would be for them to go out and do a good deed for someone else, and for them to pass it on and so on and so on… I think the human race of this day and time can open doors for tomorrow's souls. So when you've been blessed as Ms. Pattie Labelle says, "pass it on."

Behold, how good and how pleasant it is for brethren to dwell together in unity!
Psalms 133:1

*I will lift up mine eyes unto the
hills, from whence cometh my help.
My help cometh from the Lord
which made heaven and earth.*
Psalms 121:1-2

CHAPTER 8

I Wonder If God Knows About This?

You know there are so many bad things that happen in a person's lifetime, but I believe that there are just as many good things that happen. There has to be some sort of balance in life. The only thing about this theory is that we have a tendency to only remember the bad stuff that happens to us; it is like the power of the bad has a stronger hold on our minds then the good stuff that happens to us.

I believe that if you were to ask ten people to tell you five good things that happened to them from their childhood up to the present and five bad things that happened to them from their childhood up to present, and let them answer them in any order that they choose, most likely they will remember the bad things first. It's like when something good happens to us we forget it the fastest, you know like we don't retain the good memories as well as we retain the bad things. Maybe it is because when we are hurt it goes deeper to our core and our spiritual being. I know that I have been hurt so bad that I believe that if a person could see the real me from the inside, they could see the scars of hurt and all the painful things I carry around from my past.

These scars are there for a reason and that is to protect me from any future pain that may come my way. The scars tell me when to put my guard up and when to let it down. They also teach me to not let the same thing happen to me, you know like fire is hot so don't stick your hand back on it. But I don't have the same type of guard in my memories for the good things. Like something to tell me, yes, you do need to do this. Can't you remember how good you felt afterwards, so yes, let's try this again.

I can remember when I was young, one of my father's sister came to town and I knew right then I wanted to be just like her. After a period of time passed, my aunt and her family moved into her own place which was alright with me because we ended up moving just up the street from her.

Whenever things got to bad for me I would run to my aunt's place. Sometimes it seemed as if all hell was breaking loose all around me. It felt as though I would be swallowed up by the whole world, but all I had to do was to look for my aunt. You know for me to just be able to see her face and she always had this smile for me as if to say "You know I was just thinking about you" and everything that was going on around me was gone. It was like my aunt was giving me some of her strength to help me stand. It was like I didn't care how many times my step-mom would beat me. I knew that she didn't like my aunt and she didn't like for me to be around her, but to me she was worth the slaps and the beatings.

When I think back on why I loved my aunt so much it is because she was mine. She would always tell me that I was her first niece and that she was my first aunt. I had never owned anything before, nothing. Just about all of my clothes were either hand-me-downs or bought from some thrift store, and when I had worn them, they were passed down to my next sister. I didn't have my own bed or anything. But now I had something, an aunt that was mine.

When I was about ten or eleven years old, one day my uncle who was married to my aunt at the time, said to me that he needed to tell me something and he wanted to know how much he could trust me. I knew that there was bad blood between my step-mom and my aunt so I thought he needed to know if I would go back and tell my her what they were planning to do. But this uncle knew how much I wanted to be with my aunt and he used this to sexually abuse me. I can remember his words to this day.

"Your auntie really do love you. She has told me that one day she is going to take you away from here and you will never have to come back. But you need to do whatever I tell you to do to see if me and your auntie can depend on and trust you."

I don't know what happened but my dear auntie ended up leaving me behind. She would not even tell me what had gone wrong. All I can remember was that she didn't want to talk to me anymore and I was told to go back home. I went home and packed some

things into a paper bag (because back in those days
there was no plastic grocery bags) and went to sleep.
I got up early the next morning only to find out that
she had already gone. I remember crying and hiding
in the back seat of an old car that one of my mom's
new uncle had left.

I had came up with an idea that maybe my aunt
didn't know that I was not with her, and that she
would turn around and come back to get me. So I
would wait right there for her to come back for me.
No one would be able to see me from where I was,
but I could see her when she came back. But one
hour turned into two and then three and before I
knew it I had fallen asleep. I had cried myself to
sleep. It had started to get dark when I awoke. I left
the clothes in the paper bag in the car and walked
home feeling like I was lower than the dirt that I was
walking on.

When I got home the first thing that my mom did
was to knock me down to the floor with one big slap
to the back of my head. She kicked me and told me
to go in the room and take off all my clothes and to
wait for her. She whipped me till I was black and
blue all over from my head to my feet.

She says that I made it bad on myself because I
would not talk or say anything when she was
speaking to me and asking me where had I been and
who was I with? I can remember at least two weeks
had gone by before I started back talking. I was hurt
to the bones and wanted nothing to do with life any
more. All I wanted to do was to die, but not even
death wanted anything to do with me. I later over

heard my mom on the phone with one of her sisters talking about me.

"I believe she snuck out the house to be with a boy. She'll think twice before she do that again. I never did find out where she was or who she had been with. I tried to kill her."

If she only knew that at that moment I was already dead on the inside. I told myself that I was never going to love anybody, no aunts, no uncles, nobody, not even myself. I didn't even care enough to stop her from telling lies on me about being with some boy. I didn't care what anybody thought about me.

About a year had gone by when this young couple moved into our neighborhood. They had a young baby. I don't remember how we started to talk but we did and my step-mom would let me go to their place. They use to drive this really old black car. The guy loved that car. He would clean that car almost every day if he could. I started to take to them and found someone that I could talk to. The young lady would look for me every day and she would tell my step-mom that I was helping her out with her baby and she was able to get her house work done. She would ask me what I wanted to be when I grew up. She knew that I was being abused and she felt that I needed somewhere to come to and just get some rest.

We became close friends over a short amount of time, and she told me to stop thinking bad things about myself because sooner or later something really bad would happen. I didn't believe her. It was around the holidays when she told me that she would be gone for the weekend. Monday afternoon some time she would be back. She asked me to keep an eye on their place and gave me a key so that I can go inside if I needed to get away.

Monday had come and gone and by the end of that week my mom called me and told me that she needed the house key that I had for the young couple's place. At first I tried to act as though I had lost the key but she was not hearing that, so I gave in and gave it to her. She showed me a clipping from a local news paper where it showed a picture of an old car bent up. The front of the car was smashed all the way to the trunk of the car, and my step-mom said to me, "If you can read maybe you should read this because I don't think that I can make up something this bad at the drop of a hat."

I didn't know what she was going on about so I read the news paper clipping. And it said that the young couple was on holidays with the young man's family. He had gotten a family member to look after their little baby girl and the two of them went out for the evening. But the two didn't come back. The family found out that they were involved in a accident and there were no survivors.

I don't know how the story ended but I was mad at the world for taking my new friend, but then I remembered my friend had told me to stop talking about bad things all the time before something bad really does happen, and now here was something really bad. I felt like it had happened because whenever anybody got close to me something bad always happened.

My step-mom and someone else went in their house and picked over her stuff. Just seeing my mom do this made me feel that I had let my friend down again. I felt numb for days and the days turned into weeks and so on. Have you ever hurt so bad that even the hurt's hurt? I wonder if God see all of the hurts that we go through? This is why I believe that for every bad side there must be a good and happy side. If the good and bad didn't balance out the whole world would be slanted.

But I try even harder to keep fresh memories of the good thing that has happened in my past. I can remember times when I was with my father at his house. My dad had a drinking problem. If he didn't have a drink first thing in the morning he was miserable and everyone else would be miserable as well. But when he was drinking he would keep you laughing. He was everyone's pal and good friend.

One day my dad had to go to the doctor because he was starting to have problems with his stomach. So he goes to see the doctor and the doctor asked my dad a question.

"Do you have a drinking problem?"

"The only time I have a drinking problem is when I can't get a drink."

One time my dad had been drinking and all of us kids were there. It was snowing outside and the wind was blowing really hard. My dad was cooking something. I don't remember what he was cooking, but it was in a frying pan and there was a lot of hot cooking oil in the pan. He was telling us kids not to be like his girl friend. He said we should learn how to keep a man happy, and that we must cook for our man and to do whatever needs to be done to keep a happy home.

He walks through the house in a wife beater shirt and some shorts with no shoes or socks on. Then he kicks the back door and throws the hot oil out the door. The wind blew the oil right back in the door and on his legs and feet. I promise you that I have never seen a person holler so loud and jump so high. When he came back down it was like he was speaking in tongues and kicking and shouting.

I laughed and I cried till I got sick, and to this very day even though my father is no longer with us I can say that he taught me how to laugh. And there was another time I was with dad that I will never forget. He was always up to no good. I was young and I knew that by him taking me with him that it was going to be a fun day. He was driving his old red and white truck. But I didn't know where we were so I'm trying to remember the names of the roads so that if needed I could remember how to get back home.

My dad would talk to me the whole time.

"Now girl where we are going I don't want you to unlock the truck doors for nobody, not even your mama. Do you hear what I'm saying to you girl?"

"Yes sir."

So he goes out off the main highway onto a dirt road and the road is rough and dusty and long. And by now I was starting to get afraid because he kept telling me not to open the doors for any reason.

"Girl, I don't care if God himself come and tell you to open the door, what are you going to do?"

"I will not open the door," I assured him.

"Just wait for me to come back and I will take us to buy some lunch."

Now my mind is running wild and I'm thinking crazy things because I don't know what he was going to do. My dad gets out the truck and tells me to lock all of the doors, so I do as he tells me and right away he is gone from my sight. It's like he never walked away or nothing and this scared me, so much that I covered up my head with one of my dad's jackets,and started to cry.

All of a sudden I felt someone bumping and banging on the door of the truck and there was this loud hollering.

"Open the door, I said open up this**## door."

I didn't recognize the voice because my head was covered with this big old coat. The voice continued.

"You damn fool, open the door!"

I started to scream and holler. With the coat still over my head, I ducked down on the floor of the truck thinking that I was about to have a heart attack or just die from being scared to death. After a while I got up the nerves to peek from under the coat and out the window, only to see my dad rolling down a hill from where he had fallen from the start. He had landed on a wasp nest and they were stinging him like I had never seen before. He was cursing me out so bad I tell you I do believe that if he could have gotten his hands on me I wouldn't be here today.

When he did make it back up the hill he had a rock in his hand and he was trying to throw it at the window so I ducked again trying not to get hit by the rock or the broken glass. My dad finally grabbed a hold onto the door knob.

He said to me, "You little dumb b##*%, Open this #$%% door 'fore I do something to you." When I got the door open, I tell you, he was messed up. Those wasps had a field day with him.

On the way back home my dad says to me "You are one little dumb chick and you are just like that dumb monster that you live with. I could have died back there and you would have sat and done nothing. What were you thinking by not opening the door? "

I answered. "Well, daddy, you said not to open the doors, not even for God."

"Girl, don't ever tell anybody that, OK. It's got to be something wrong with you and don't think that I am buying you anything to eat now, because when I was trying to steal some of the white man's weed, you let me down. And now just look at me."

Oh my God, to this very day I can see him rolling up and down that hill cursing me out and all I can do is laugh until I cry.

When I sit back and remember the things that have happened to me, sometimes I cry and other times I laugh as if it just happened. I know that we tend to only remember who hurt us and how they did it and some of the hurts are as fresh as the day that it actually happened.

We have the ability to recall agony and pain from somewhere deep inside but I don't think that God wanted it to be this way. I have been reading the Bible now for some years but I don't claim to know everything. As long as I have been reading the word of God I have not seen anywhere where it says that we are to hold on to the bad things that happened to us. Now I have read where the word of God says that we are to forgive and it also says that we are to love one another.

Have you ever known someone who is just straight out evil? I am not talking about a regular unsaved person. There is a difference. First you have your everyday person who don't go to church and whatever the reason has not accepted Christ Jesus as his or her own personal Savior. I don't have a problem with this person and their beliefs. Yes, I have more respect for a person who is truthful with themselves and most always do what is right.

Now the other person that I am talking about is someone who just doesn't care about anybody but themselves. This person will lie, cheat and steal and don't care about you or me or anybody else. They seem to get away with everything. You may not believe me when I tell you that I know a person like this. She will steal from a baby and not feel bad about it, and if you were to ask her about it (and I have) she will say, "Oh you know that that child didn't need that," I would tell her, "You know that was wrong and you should be ashamed of yourself."

They drink smoke and curse and just don't care about anyone. Even when the law gets involved with them it is as if they are so slippery that they are able to get out of everything. It is like the devil himself has trained them. And this person that I knew when I was young, I would just sit back to see what was going to be the next thing that she was going to do and do you know I never had to wait long. She never failed to do something more rotten then the time before.

She always got what she wanted. She would sit back and plot and plan on who to rob next. She didn't care if the person needed to pay their rent or needed food and that was all that they had in life, she just didn't care. I remember thinking why is it that she never goes without, and everyday it seems as though she could find someone to steal from. I use to pray that the police would arrest her and keep other people safe from her, but she would go down town to jail and the very next day she was back saying that she got time served or that one of her friends had bonded her out. She would never show up to court or anything. Now where is the justice in this, I ask you. Here this person is doing anything and everything and nothing bad ever happens to them and I know that she is not the only one doing this.

So I ask you, does God really see this? I also know this other person who truly believes in God. She is saved and is in church every time the doors open. She works hard and gives her last to help someone who has less than her. She does not drive a big car nor does she live a glorious life style. In fact her lights are often turned off for non-payment and her water bill is almost always over due. But she prays and smiles and keeps her head high and tries to get a break in life only to keep getting knocked back down.

This friend of mine went to work one day and the place was robbed and she was hurt and could not afford to go to the hospital, but she went anyway because she was hurt. When she came back to work she found out that she had been fired for not finishing her shift. Now what is life showing her? Does God see this? I wonder does He know about this?

I know that sometimes it doesn't seem as though God is watching us with all of the things that we go through, but I would rather believe that he is near and his hands are keeping me from falling. And God didn't promise us that every day was going to be sunshine. There has got to be some rain sometimes, and if we didn't have hard times in our lives how then can we appreciate the good times?

Thus saith the Lord unto you, be not afraid nor dismayed by reason of this great multitude; for the battle is not yours, but God's.
11Chronicles 20:15

My son, if your heart is wise , my heart will rejoice- indeed, I myself;
Yes, my inmost being will rejoice when your lips speak right things.
Proverbs 23:15-16

Ah Lord God! Behold , thou hast made the heaven and the earth by thy great power and stretched out arm, and there is nothing too hard for thee.

Jeremiah 32:17

CHAPTER 9

If It's Done in the Dark, Will it Come to Light?

I can remember getting to meet my maternal great grandmother and not just her but a large amount of my family from both of my parents sides of their family. Since I didn't know my family as a child, it was kind of hard to learn everyone as a young adult. In fact, a lot of the relationships that I did have were strained and they felt forced and unreal, like when the lights were on everybody was happy to see each other and when the lights were off nobody wanted you to be in their space.

And for this reason I didn't feel the need to try to get to know or to meet any more of them, and to this very day I still don't know a lot of my family members. I arrived with no money, no car, and very few clothes. Because of my condition, the first thing that the family was saying is "What does she want? And where is she going to live?" So I can say that not everyone was happy to see me. The exception was my great grandmother, who was the most real person that I ever met. She would tell me to come closer to her so that she didn't have to raise her voice because she was not talking to the whole house, and to me, this was deep.

When she did speak to me, I never once thought to question her truthfulness. She had this way about her that made me feel extremely welcome and at ease with her. Whenever she would start to tell me something it was as if I was right there as it was happening and I could see it as the stories unfolded in front of me.

"Now sister" she would say to me, "I don't care what you do in the dark, it will come to light. If you cover your feet then your head will show, and if you cover your head your feet will show."

"What do you mean, grandma?" I asked.

"It means don't ever do anything that you don't want no one to know about, because someone will always see what you are doing. You may not even know the person but they will know somebody that you know."

Grandma would tell me that I was a young lady and not just a woman. I asked her to explain the difference.

"Well, a young woman will go out and do anything and everything that she is big enough to do and it won't matter to her one way or another. But a young lady will only do what is seemingly right. No one would be able to say bad things about her or judge how her family raised her. The young lady would be concerned about how her actions would reflect on her family but the young woman would not care nor have any shame. The young woman only wants to do what makes her feel good for right now." She would say to me that I was a young lady and not just a woman. I asked her to explain the difference in a young lady and a young woman. She said that a young woman will go out and do anything and everything that she is big enough to do and it won't matter to her one way or another. But a young lady will only do what is seemingly right. No one would be able to say bad things about her or judge how her family raised her. The young lady would be concerned about how her actions would reflect on her family but the young woman would not care or have any shame. The young woman only wants to do what makes her feel good for right now.

After she told me this I sat and thought on the subject for a while. I asked her about the young man.

"Oh, you don't have to worry about a young man because you will never be a man, young or old. So just concern yourself with how to be a young lady, okay?"

I could tell that she knew that I wasn't satisfied with that answer. She explained further.

"Do you know that if a woman were to go out and take off all her clothes and walk in the parking lot down there that everybody and their mama's mamas will be talking about her, even if there was someone who didn't see it, they will have heard about it."

She said that if a young man were to do the same thing, folks would talk about it today, but come tomorrow folks will be talking about something else.

I asked my great grandmother why is it that people do things like this and she said to me "Now who are you asking, all I know is if you keep on living you will find out that what I am telling you is true, or either you will find out what is the matter with people, but if I were you I wouldn't waste any time trying to figure out why people for hundreds and hundreds of years do what it is that people do."

She also told me "If I had that much time on my hands to wonder about the things that other folks do then I must be neglecting something else that needs to be done."

During the little amount of time that I had to share with my great grandmother I could always depend on her to tell me the gospel truth about any and everything and if she didn't know, then guess what, she would tell me that she didn't know. She wasn't one of those persons who held anything back because it hurt your feelings, and she always said that the truth hurts.

She called me one day and said to me "You know sister, (she started calling me sister late one night and I don't know why but this was her new name for me) people are going to talk about you no matter what you do, and some is going to be true and other times it will not, and if it hurts you by what they are saying just don't pay it any attention. Now if it is true what they are saying and it hurts, then you need to pay it some attention and fix whatever it is, but if it isn't broken then don't fix it. Don't you ever let the devil ride with you or soon he will want to drive, in other words be careful of who you entertain."

Not everyone who has a smile on their face is going to be your friend. Sometimes folk will try to find out all of your business just to have something to talk about with someone else.

I know by now you may be saying, "Why is she just talking about her great grandmother"? The answer is that she was a remarkable person. I was blessed to have met her. For the short time that I had her in my life, it was life-changing for me. As the years go by I can still see her and hear her in every aspect of my life. And I do give her all the credit for me being here today, and for the frame of mind that I have today.

Because I truly do believe that the devil had a plan for me, but James 5:16 tells us to *"Confess your trespasses to one another, and pray for one another, that you may be healed. The effective, fervent prayer of righteous man avails much."*

I now know that my great grandmother's prayer saved me, because I can remember asking everyone that I came in contact with was I going crazy? One time I asked my great grandmother if I was going crazy, and she said to me, "Sister, out of all the places that you can go, why go there"? She told me that if I found that I had to go crazy then don't stay there long because I might not be able to find my way back.

I remember one evening I was sitting around just listening to my great grandmother reminiscing on her life. She asked me why I take life so seriously. I didn't understand what it was that she was asking me about, so I shrugged my shoulders and said, "I don't know what you want me to say." At that point there was so much going on in my life and I was not in control of anything.

Everything and everyone that was a part of my life was gone. I had to make a decision whether to go backwards in life and try to climb out of the hole and the mess that my life had become, or go forward and pick my life up and try to make something out of it. Sometimes when we are down and out, we start to think that there is only one other way to go and that is up, but that is not so because if you stay down and out you can find yourself looking death right in the face. If you don't do something about your situation, all kind of things will start to go wrong in your life.

Now here I was staying with a family that knew nothing about me and I knew even less about them, and everyone had something going on in their lives and not to mention the fact that everyone was into church. I had been to church maybe five times in my adult life. I didn't know why everyone was so happy about church and God and everything else that came along with it, and just what was it that they was expected of me. This meant that I had no kind of relationship with God. Even though I had been bought up in a church, I can't remember one time ever reading a Bible.

During my life I could remember praying to a God that I thought was somewhere else. Hey, I felt that God was anywhere that I wasn't. Why? Because out of all the years that I had been talking to him, nothing good had ever happened for me, so I believed that he didn't know me. The only thing I knew about him was that he didn't want anything to do with me.

I was on my own in a world full of kin folks. I felt as if I was an island and all of the kin folks were the water that surrounded me. The way things were going for me, it was high tides which meant that I was under water swallowed up and had become to be no more. I felt as though I had become a failure at the ripe old age of twenty-three.

When I tell you that I have seen down and out and it isn't a pretty sight, you might say that most young people are just getting started in life. But here I was throwing in the towel and ready to call it quits. So this is why I felt as though I couldn't answer my great grandmother's question about taking life so seriously.

I took a moment to think on all that had been going on in my life. I had not long ago given birth to my son for whom I was in no shape to care for. I had to make a decision to give him up for adoption. And here was my great grandmother asking me why I was being so serious. Hmmm. Let me see, what else was I thinking about. I couldn't see what it was that she was saying to me.

In fact, I had started to think that maybe, just maybe, my great grandmother was starting to forget who it was that she was talking to. So I said to her, "You know, if it weren't for bad luck I'd have no luck at all, and you are asking me this. What else is there to think happy thoughts about?" I can remember how she laughed when I said this to her, and I started to wonder if I had missed something. I thought about all that had happened and tried to figure out what had I missed.

For the life of me I couldn't figure it out so I said to her, "Is there some other way I need to see things? What is in life to be so happy about"?

She said to me, "Now sister, I know good and well that you can find something in this world to be happy about even if it is just for a little while. You've had a couple of things to go wrong and now even the good things looked bad to you."

I could not believe what I was hearing so I asked her to please tell me what it was that I had missed. Even though I knew that she knew that I was being negative she entertained me anyway.

"Look at you. You have your health and strength. Oh, I believe that's enough to be grateful for all by itself. Sister, I have been praying for you a long time. I don't know if I will ever see you again. Every time you prayed for death to come to you, I prayed for God to keep you in his healing hands."

She said that she didn't know where I was or what was going on with me but she did know that God had his hand in my life. Even if I didn't know him she knew that he did know me. She said to me again, "Oh, I believe that's enough right there to be grateful for."

As I sat there listening to her go on and on she said to me, "Sister, you asked God to enable you to meet your mother and he did it for you. Just because things didn't go as you wanted to, you became blinded to your gift and called it a curse."

"What is my gift?"

"Your mother is young and healthy and so are you."

That meant that there was time for us to have the kind of relationship that I wanted and we both needed. My grandmother told me to stop seeing everything as something else bad that was happening to me and that I must start looking for the good that would be in my trials. I can hear her saying "Sister not all trials have to come with tribulation."

She said that I had so much to be thankful for and didn't even know it, and by now I knew that I wanted to know what she knew. I ask her how am I able to do this when everything that I touched never worked out for my good. The only good thing that had ever happened to me was that she had come into my life, and I told her that I was afraid that something would go wrong with that too.

"What could ever go wrong with the two of us"?

"Well, for starters, someone might find out that my mom was not my real mom and then that would mean that you didn't have to care about me anymore."

"Sister, you may not know that she is your real mother, but I know it. Until you find out for yourself you don't need to trouble yourself, because I know it for the both of us."

My great grandmother laughed so hard that she started to cough, so I said, "Or I could cause you to laugh and cough yourself to death."

"There is no such luck of that happening because we know who you are even though you don't know who you are," she said to me.

I didn't get as much time with her as I wanted, but even in her death she still teaches me life's lessons, and one of them is I can love and that I did and still to this very day love her and miss her. She showed me unconditional love. The type of love that she showed me I had never seen or heard of before so it made me afraid. I thought that it was too good to be true.

Instead of me spending every moment that I could with her I took it for granted that she would always be there. But I am grateful for being blessed to have had the amount of time with her that I did. I am forever blessed and my life will never be the same. At the time I didn't see her for what she was. Believe it or not when I say to you, God sent me an angel." Because after I had been blessed with my great grandmother, I wanted to live and I wanted to be the very best that I could be. She introduced me to God.

She showed me that with God all things are possible, and that if I included God into everything that I do in life then things won't always go bad for me. For this alone, it was worth seeking him. I try never to take anyone for granted because most of the time God has sent them to me for a reason and it is up to me to find the blessing in everyone that I come in contact with. I may not like everyone but I do find something about them to learn.

Now I don't want you to think that my great grandmother doesn't live on. Every time I see my grandmother I see her. Sometime when I'm on the phone with grandmother and she laughs, I have to remind myself that it is not great-grandmother. She may be gone but I can tell you that she will never be forgotten.

One day I was visiting my mother. I don't know why to this very day my mom called me "sister" and I froze. I had to turn and look twice before I could move. Maybe my mother did it to see the look that would be on my face, or just to get a laugh, I don't know.

I have learned not to dwell on all of life's mishaps. If they are there to become a stumbling block, it is up to me not to allow it to happen. I try not to see it as a stumbling block, but as a challenge. I now see them as being blocks to elevate me up higher to bigger and better things. I know now that my great grandmother spoke words of encouragement into my life and into my spirit and to me. When she found me I was at my lowest point in life, so she not only shared words of encouragement but she planted seeds of life.

Have you ever planted a garden and as time goes by a plant springs forth. After that some weeds will also start to grow. If you don't keep the weeds out of your garden they will choke out your plants and kill them. Now, I don't know about you but sometimes I will get an idea and start to do a new task and just like that I would stop doing it and start something else. I can't start to count the number of things that I have started and they never did get finished.

That old devil will kill every idea that you are blessed with, but only if we allow him to. You also have to water and fertilize your garden so that your plants will become healthier. Invest in your dreams because if you don't take any action your dreams will never become reality; they will always remain just a dream. So if you want the good stuff to grow then you must take care of it, which means spending time and energy in it. Even then you must guard against the birds and the bugs that will come along and eat the plants. There are so any things that can hinder your plants from growing.

Don't ever give up on yourself, because if you don't invest back into your dreams then who else will. This is what my great grandmother did for me, She invested into me even when I couldn't see why. I don't know what it was that she saw in me and I don't know if anybody else could see it but she didn't say what do you need from me, all she said was you are going to live and you are going to do it either by walking or you going to be pulled, one way or the other. She had her own set ways about doing things, and more than likely you would never even know what it is that she was doing until after it was already done.

Whenever I get a chance to talk with my grandmother about my great grandmother, we hardly ever run out of things to say about her, and I find out more and more about her. I will often start to tell my grandmother about something that my great grandmother and I had talked about and she will say to me "Did she tell you about that too?" or she will tell me about how my great grandmother was always there for her.

She told me that my great-grandmother didn't ever halfway do things. She always went above and beyond the norm. Whatever she gave, she gave wholeheartedly. Whenever her names comes up in conversation, I look at the faces of my family members and I see the sides of their mouth curl up unto a smile. A look comes across their faces as if they're saying, "If only you could imagine what she means to me." I think that my great grandmother in her own way inspired each of her children, and her children's children. As for me I will forever cherish my great grandmother. Because of her, my life will never be the same, and I am eternally grateful for her.

I pray that this chapter finds a special place in your heart and that you too will be able to grow into your blessing as well. And please look into your own family and draw strength from them, and also be the strength that they need as well. And let your light shine, because it may be someone down in the valley trying to get home.

Trust in the Lord with all thine heart; and lean not unto thine own understanding..
Proverbs 3:5

Withhold not correction from the child: for if thou beatest him with the rod, he shall not die. Thou shall beat him with the rod, and shall deliver his soul from hell.

CHAPTER 10

Who is Allowed to the Family Cook Out?

When I was a little kid growing up in the north we didn't get to have many cook outs for several reasons. It wasn't because it was always cold. First, we were not all located in the same area. Second, nobody got along long enough to know who was cooking what and where.

Back then no one said that they didn't eat pork or meat or whatever. If you were hungry, you ate whatever was cooked, but I did hear my aunt say that she would rather starve to death than eat some of my other aunt's cooking. Once I even heard them say this about my step-mom, so in order for me to hear what was being said I would walk slow, acting like I had to go to the bathroom.

I overheard my grand-mom say that my step-mom was nasty and who does she think is going to eat her cooking? And one of the older aunts said that some of the men that my step-mom went with looked like something that you would find on skid row. She said that the kind of men my step-mom liked were the ones that needed to be cleaned up because they were a mess. My grand-mom said that my step-mom had no standards whatsoever in a man. She also said that the only qualification that a man needed to get with my step-mom was to have a dollar in his pockets. She didn't look at the man's face or how he carried himself; the only thing that she saw was his pockets and how much money was in them.

Grand-mama said that since my step-mom lay down with the dogs, she got up with fleas. She said the men that my step-mom went out with smelled bad and looked nasty. They wondered what in the world she saw in them.

My grand-mom took a pot of food that my aunt had cooked and brought with her to the cookout and she gave it to my cousin and told her to put it back in the bag that it had came in and try not to let it fall into the trash can. They said that my aunt had bad roaches, and the roaches would be in the bags that she brought the food in and there were times that the roaches were in the food.

I thought about what they were saying and it came to me that my family is not very bright at all and that they were "country" and couldn't help themselves. First of all if a person has roaches how can you tell if the roaches are bad or good, you know what I'm saying? A roach is a roach.

The older women would say that they didn't eat one of my younger cousin's cooking. I couldn't hear why at first because when they saw me coming in the house all of them stopped talking until I had left the room, but I knew that they would start back talking again once I was out of the room.

I went and sat down in the living room pretending to watch TV until they started to talk again. I didn't want to turn the sound down on the TV so I had to strain to hear what was being said about this cousin. I couldn't hear her name, but I could hear them say that she (the younger cousin) was nasty and did anyone see how she was dressed. One of my aunts said that she had gone to the younger cousin's house and she was just getting out of bed. She went straight into the kitchen without washing her face or anything and started to cook, so she knew for sure that she was nasty.

So with all of this that was going on we never did know who was speaking to whom and why not. It never did fail that somebody was mad at someone else, and if they weren't speaking to each other then guess what, they weren't eating anybody's cooking either. I don't know if your family is anything like mine but if the adults were not talking then the kids were not supposed to be talking either.

Now in our family it was the golden rule for the kids not to be in grown-ups business. We were not allowed to speak to whomever our parents didn't speak to not knowing why we were not speaking or how long the spat was going to last. That also means that the kids were now into grown-ups business. We kids were made to be mad with each other as well, even though we didn't get to see or to spend much time with our cousins as it was. Now we weren't allowed to play with each other.

I don't know what we were mad about but not being able to play with each other was enough reasons for us to be mad. Sometimes we would be mad for so long that when we did see our kin folks us kids would have to check it out with our parents to see if they were the ones that we weren't suppose to be talking to. Sometimes our whole family would end up mad with everybody.

One week some of our family members would side with each other so that there would end up being different groups going against each other. It became so confusing and out of control that people other than our family thought that we were gang members. We didn't have certain colors we wore, nor did we have certain territories, but we had something different from all of that kind of stuff. We had the church folks and their kids on one side and the alcoholic and the mishaps and their kids on the other side. The only problem with this for our family was that one week we were on the church folk's side and the next week we were on the alcoholic's side.

My step-mom was saved on Sundays (saved from what I don't know) and from Monday through Saturday she let her hair down and everything else, and whatever the church people didn't do she did do it. You can see why we children didn't know if we were going or coming. One week we were getting a whipping for speaking to our family members and the next week we were getting whippings for being disrespectful for not speaking to them.

If you say you are having a cookout, most people would probably think of a barbecue, right? but not my kin folks. In fact, during my whole childhood I can't remember our family ever having more than two barbecues, and the first one was when we kids and some of the neighbor kids were playing around in our yard and we started to get hungry. We knew it was late in the day and if we went in we would have to stay inside, so we came up with the idea to build ourselves a barbecue grill.

Now you may not believe it when I tell you this but everything that we needed to build this grill was right there in our yard. My step-mom was a carpenter and a tailor and a hair stylist. Yep, you name it and she did it. She liked to say she was a jack of all trades and a master of none. So this was why we had all sorts of stuff just laying around our yard. To tell you the truth I can't ever remember my step-mom ever buying any of the lumber or the cinder blocks, or the nails and the other tools that she had laying around the house. I guess that is something to think about.

So as I was saying we built this grill and to keep from having to go into the house we went to the store to get some hot dogs and bread and some drinks. There was this guy named Mr. Ervin that ran a barbershop and out of the barbershop he ran a store. My dad would go to Mr. Ervin to get his hair cut and sometimes a shave. My dad told Mr. Ervin to let us (his kids) get something from his store to snack on and to put it on his tab and he would pay it whenever he came in for his next hair cut. We had thought of everything but how we were going to light the grill and how to cook our hot dogs, so we had to get an adult to help us with this, but in the end it all worked out alright.

The next barbecue that we had was for my graduation from high school. This was some years between the hot dog and the graduation barbecue. In fact, my step-mom cooked for two days. I thought that she was being nice to me by doing all that cooking and come to find out she was up to no good as usual. She told my dad that she was throwing me a cookout in order for him to give her some money to buy her and our new uncle and their friends some beer and liquor.

The next day after the cook out we found out that the cookout was for her new boy-friend's birthday, and when my dad heard about what she had done and confronted her about it she came up with the story that since I had graduated on the same day as her boy friend's birthday, she just made it into one big party. But instead of the cake saying "Congratulations for graduating," it said "How Old Are You"?

Everyone just thought that instead of her having a cake made for me, that she must have been on a budget and that she must have gotten a better deal on a left over cake that someone didn't show up to get or something like that. We didn't know that she had told her boy friend that the party was for him in order for him to give her some money as well, which she didn't spend all on the party. You know, we should have known that something was not right. For starters, I didn't drink neither did the people that she allowed me to invite. Most of us were either still in school or just graduating from school, and the second thing was that over half of the people that were there I had never seen in my whole life.

Whenever someone would ask my step-mom who were those people she would say, "Don't worry about them because they are my friends from out of town and I invited them. God knows that there is more than enough food. I don't know when they will get to come back to town to see me."

When my dad or someone that knew my dad asked her about them and where they came from, she would tell them that they were there to play the music for the cookout.

I tell you this much, for a person who says that she hates anyone who tell lies she must really hate herself because she was a pro at lying. I believe that she could get paid for some of the stuff that she came up with. She was so good at lying that she could have done the movie of the week and have part one and a part two and if the pay was right she could keep them coming.

And the bad part about her telling you a lie was that you would know that she wasn't being truthful with you and she would make you feel like either you must have forgotten something that she had said or either you just weren't paying any attention to what she had told you. I promise you that she would leave you scratching your head after a conversation with her, and whenever she was caught she would beat you getting mad and curse you out as if you had done something to her. I believe that she alone was the reason why headache medicine was made and she has probably kept a lot of the companies in business by giving people headaches.

As everyone started to figure out the confusion that my step-mom had caused, it didn't take long before she came up with a different story for anyone who wanted to know what happened. If you were one that checked out what she had said with someone else, guess what, you were now one of the family members that we were not allowed to talk to any more. So now the cookout was over and this was the end of the barbecues as I know it.

When I got older and moved to the south, I was staying with my father's family. When they had their family gathering it was a whole different story. And one thing about it is that they call it a get together, or a family reunion. This always threw me off because when you look up the word reunion in Webster's dictionary it says that it is a coming together again of something or someone. So how can anything re-unite if it wasn't ever together from the start?

I had never seen most of the family that was there and it wasn't just me, because I met some family who said that they were there to find out who was family, because they didn't want to end up dating or having kids with someone that was in the family.

Now when my family has a cookout one person will get on the phone and start calling around to find out who is coming and what they are bringing. They would tell everyone where to meet and what time to be there. You had to bring what you said you were bringing and make sure it was enough for everyone.

Now if you don't want any trouble with everyone else you are not to bring any guest with you other than your kids and your spouse, because my aunts would let you know right from the start that nobody was there to try to feed everybody. And

God forbid if something were to come up and you are not able to get what it is that you are supposed to bring to the cookout. Cause nobody got extra money just laying around the house or wherever it is that you may stay to buy what you didn't bring.

Most of my family is already robbing Peter to pay Paul, and for someone to put you down to bring something to a cookout, how are you supposed to come up with your part. So I know what you are thinking; then don't bring anything, right? Wrong. The other family will talk about you until the cows come home, and not only will they talk about you but they will watch you the whole time that you are there to see if you are going to eat what someone else has bought.

So even if you decide not to come, they will have something to say about this, too. So, you really can't win for losing because they will say that they had to go without something because you didn't bring what it was that you were to bring.

Even if everything goes well and you do bring what you promised to bring, there is still going to be somebody who will be watching how much food that everyone is putting on their plates. So do you see what it is that I'm saying? You can't win for losing.

Now I don't know how certain family members are put in charge of telling who is allowed to come to the family cookouts and who is not, but whoever it is, turns out that they don't ask everybody for their opinion because it almost never fails that someone is going to bring somebody that was not invited, and this will bring on the attitudes. And for this very reason I don't attend any of the cookouts that are held by my family. Not all of my family is like this. I don't want anyone to get the wrong idea of my family. I think that we all have some members of our family who are like this.

Now I attend family cookouts with my mother's side of the family. Whenever my family has a cookout, it is an unwritten law that everyone must meet up at my mother's for dinner. You could have been up all night cooking for your company to come over, but if they plan on spending some time with you or your household, then they better make it a brunch because dinner time the whole house has got to be shut down to go to my mother's for dinner. If you are going to be late that still is not a problem because my mother has her own committee that will track you down.

I have often said that if I were ever blessed with a large amount of money that I would not buy my mother a car or gold or even diamonds, because I really don't believe that she would enjoy it as much as having a large kitchen to cook in. She doesn't even have to have a large place to feed all of the people that come to her house for dinner. I believe that she and my step-father could open up and run a catering business. The only problem with this is that she wouldn't get paid for the food because she will have given it all away.

There must be a calling or something going on in her life because she gets such great joy just to feed folks. Now I don't know if my step-father has the same calling, but just from being with my mother he could make a great chef and a short order cook. He can also prep food as well. I believe that the two of them are like the story in the Bible that all they would need is two fish and five loaves of bread to feed everybody that comes there to eat. Between the two of them on a Sunday, they could feed five thousand, and don't come around on a holiday; they could feed a multitude.

Do you know that church people are forever telling that Jesus was the son of a carpenter, and that Jesus is the son of God, but nobody ever tells how good of a restaurant owner he could have been. If you don't believe me, just look in your Bible. Go over to the book of Matthew in the 14th chapter or the 8th chapter of Mark where it tells of Jesus feeding five thousand people with two fish and five loaves of bread. And how about where Jesus turns water into wine in the book of John 2:3. Now who couldn't make it with him. I can tell you that a five star restaurant has got nothing on him. And if you want to give him credit, then how about Jesus was the one who started the all-you-can-eat places.

I don't care how many buffets that you come up with, nobody you know of can feed that many people on the budget that he did and still had leftovers for a doggie bag. I am going to stop saying that before somebody gets offended, but there have been times when everyone would be eating and one of my little brother's ex's will be there and then one of his "right now's" show up and I must say that all eyes will be following them to see what the outcome will be. It seems to me that when my mother cooks, her food seems to draw out all the ex's while all of the "right now's" are there.

I don't know how my mother and step-father handle it. Maybe when the grace is said for the food that instead of praying for the food that everyone has prayed for unity. I can just imagine everyone saying to themselves "Oh Lord, can't we all just get along?" As that person leaves, everyone says to them "I thank you, Lord."

My family goes through the motion just as the rest of my family does. In fact as I think back on my other family members. I believe that I was being prepared for how to handle my extended family. You know with in-laws you have to be ready at all times for a throw down with them, because somebody is going to rub somebody the wrong way and even though you will tell yourself that you are not going to get involved with whatever may be going on, I promise you that every time you will find yourself right in the middle of it. Somebody is going to have one too many drinks or not enough to drink, but either way it's going down.

When you get there nobody will ever say what is on their minds but you just stick around long enough. You won't have to wonder what is being said behind your back, because the power of alcohol has never failed. I don't know why but it always turns out to be the same person that started the last throw down at the last cookout. It's like that person comes into the house and gets a drink and starts working where they left off from the fight before.

I have a sister in-law that I don't care how much she drinks the dumber she gets. One time she got into an argument and she wanted to cut whoever it was that she was arguing with, and everyone was trying to get the knife from her and calm her down. I can never understand how she can get so messed up and never spill her drink.

I remember one time she was so messed up and mad that she was going to call the police on someone and she asked "What is the number for 911?" That's when you know you've had too much to drink.

And one time one of my sister's baby's daddy showed up with one of his girl friends, and the woman didn't like my sister in-law, but she came along to watch the baby's daddy, of whom my sister in-law could not stand. This guy didn't pay child support nor did he try to help her with his kids. This dude wouldn't even try to work because he didn't want any of his money to be taken out for his kids. He wasn't invited to the cookout out; he just heard other family members saying that they were coming to the cookout.

Now can I ask you this: Who is allowed to the family cookout?

I pray that when you have your next cook out that everyone will be invited to it ....

Behold, I stand at the door, and knock: if any man hear my voice, and open the door, I will come in to him, and will sup with him, and he with me.
Revelation 3:20

*Pray without ceasing, in everything
give thanks; for this is the will of God
in Christ Jesus for you.*
I Thessalonians 5:17-18

CHAPTER

Stained for Life

When the time came for me to start this chapter the first two attempts I became very ill. I am not talking about a head ache or a stomach ache; if it were only that or one of the two of them I could take something for it and be able to continue on with my writing, but this time it seemed to me that every part of my body was throbbing and aching.

I can remember turning on the television and it was on a Christian station and two people were praying for different things and at first I wasn't paying any attention to what they were saying. Have you ever been that kind of sick where you can't pinpoint exactly where it is that you are hurting?

But in the back ground of my mind I could hear the woman praying and saying that "Someone is being healed from arthritis in their hands," and I said hey, that's me and I started to listen on and then the man that was praying with the woman says that "Someone is being cured of a knee problem," and again I said hey, that is me too, then the woman came back and said that she sees healing of somebody's foot. Now I kid you not, I claimed that as well.

By now they had my fullest attention and out of nowhere my niece calls me.

"Auntie, how are you feeling today?"

"I am sick and trying to get a healing from the television."

"Oh, my God, auntie. You need to just call your doctor. You have been putting it off for too long."

So in order for me to get her off the phone so that I could finished claiming my healings I told her okay, first thing Monday morning.

When she hung up, I started to pray with the people on the TV. I am telling you this and I promise you on everything that I own that a small voice came out of nowhere saying " You have got to start back eating because with the kind of medication that you're on you have to eat," I had taken it upon myself to lose some weight in order for me to get off some of the medicines that I was taking.

I didn't discuss it with my doctor first. I just told myself that it was about self-discipline. I would eat at seven a.m. and seven p.m. and no foods in between. I was only drinking fluids. I said to the small voice that "If I could get some kind of confirmation I would stop what I was doing."

I had forgotten all about what had happened as I was about to take some pain medicines. I told my husband what had happened and he laughed at it (this man has been my leaning tower for over twenty-something years). Just as I was speaking about it, my mother called me. It wasn't strange for her to call me but it was out of the blue.

"How is it going"?

"I am not feeling well."

"What do you mean? Where are you not feeling well at"?

"I don't know. It feels like it is everywhere."

Then I told her about what I had been doing and how long I had been doing it. She told me I had to eat. Afterwards the whole conversation came back to me and I said, "Thank you for my confirmation, Lord!"

So here I am now writing chapter eleven. When I came up with the title for this chapter I was thinking about the different bad things that happen in our lives. The stain in this chapter is just another word for pains and heartaches and every bad thing that has ever happened to us in life. Sometimes we are hurt by the very people that we love and trust and we believe that they will protect us from harm's way, and other times we are hurt by strangers and I don't want to leave it out that sometimes we even hurt ourselves.

We find it hard sometimes to put the hurts behind us. It is so hard to let go of the pain. Which means that we haven't forgiven people for hurting us or we haven't forgiven our self, so there is no healing there. When there is no healing we can't grow in our spiritual walk. I have found out that whenever I don't deal with something bad that has happened to me immediately, it only comes back up at a later time.

It's like it gets buried somewhere in the back of my mind only to pop back up over and over again. Until I settle whatever the problem is, I will never get any rest from it. But when the problem is settled, not only will I get rest from it I will get clarity and just maybe I can learn a lesson from it. That's growth.

I tend to find that whenever a person can't forgive and the bad things continue to happen that the layers of pain just keep adding on and on until it starts to weigh a person down. This will cause a person's feeling to become dull and when something good does happen to them because of the dullness they are not able to enjoy it. Sometimes we have been hurt so often that when something good does happen to us we don't even notice it.

This dullness will cause the person to not be able to enjoy life. Over a period of time so much resentment will consume their well-being, and sooner or later they will become sick. Stress is the doorway to many illnesses, mental and physical.

Do you know that we spend more time griping and complaining than we do giving God the glory and praises?

You know I believe that if someone were to use a scale and put on one side all of our bickering, moaning, and complaining, and on the other side all of our worshiping, praising and glorifying which one do you believe will outweigh the other. I know that I fall short with my praises; the scale won't even start to balance out.

If it were me, and a person were to gripe and complain to me all the time and I knew that I had been nothing but good to them, I would feel that person was being ungrateful and didn't deserve anything else from me. What I am saying is that this person is me, and I am quicker to complain about the bad stuff that happens than I am to give thanks for all the good stuff. I have a tendency to expect bad things instead of good things to happen. I don't care what the situation is, I will always picture it going wrong. I will think about what is the worst thing that can happen, instead of thinking positive and claiming victory over my situations.

We get one or two mishaps in the run of a day and we start throwing in the towel. We need other folks to feel remorse for us. We want the whole world to stop and stand still for us to get off. We have trained ourselves to over react at the first inkling of trouble. But when I read about Job in the Bible, I see where Job was a broken man who lost almost everything that he had in a short period of time, and he still praised God and trusted and believed that God would bring him out of his state of brokenness.

Job was sick so long that his flesh fell from his bones, and even though he was being tempted and tried, he never stopped believing that God would deliver him and make him whole again. Job had faith. Even when all looked extremely devastating, he never lost his belief or faith in God. Job was told that his children and cattle and his workers all were dead, and it seemed as though nothing good was ever going to happen for him. He even cursed the day that he was born, but never did he curse God.

It was as if he was standing alone as he was going through his hardship because his wife told him to go on and curse his God and die. His long-time friends were not willing to help hold him up as he went through. All they wanted to know was what had he done to anger God, because all they ever knew of Job was that he tried to stay in God's grace. You imagine how it must have been for Job to not have anyone to confide in. You know how we can be, we need someone to tell our story to, someone who will say that they understand. Job knew that his friends were thinking and saying that he was being punished for something and he wasn't telling them about it.

I have thought about the foul things that have stained my life. Like when I was twelve, something devastating happened to me that would change my whole life. I became pregnant from a member of my step-mom's family and she beat me almost to the point of death, it was as though she thought that I wanted something like this to happen to me.

I remember every time she saw me, she would say how bad I made her family look and that she couldn't remember why she ever kept me around. You see, it is things like that that only God can bring you back from. He showed me how to go and live, and not only to just live but to want to live not just for me but a child, too.

All of the things that were going on in my life I could look back over it with such clarity. The pain was so fresh and sharp as if it had just happened this very moment. But God started to put people in places who would be there for me. My life became a puzzle and all the pieces that I had, I could not see a clear picture. I finally realized that I could not do this on my own because only more bad things were happening. I got tired of being the victim; I knew I needed someone to help me and that someone was

God. God has put some of his own pieces of my puzzle in and now I can see some great things in store for me.

God has smoothed out a lot of the bad places and now even they don't look so bad. God has always been holding me up even when I thought I was alone. That which was meant to break me has indeed made me stronger. Now I can't tell you when or where I found God, but I can tell you that he has always had me.

Whenever we go through anything big or small we call on everybody to cry on their shoulder, but after a while even that starts to get old and that shoulder starts to get farther and farther apart. And soon whenever that person sees you are hears from you all they will want to do is get away from you, because they will know that here comes you and your problems again. Some of us have worn out our friendship with all of our drama.

We sometimes become too needy and this can become a bit too stressful on a friendship. Sometimes we think that we can trust a person because we have been there for them and because we have known this person for a number of years and we tell them everything about our personal business. We think that they will never betray our trust in them only to find out that everything we have confided in this person has become public knowledge. We find out that our friendship is a little one sided. You may be best friends with this person but that doesn't mean that you are their best friend.

We have got to learn how to stop running to people whenever trouble arises. We need to learn how to cope with things and to handle our own situations. I don't know about you but I would like to know that I can be a problem solver if I need to be. How can we be there for someone else if we don't know how to handle our own day to day problems?

I like to believe that I have a close enough relationship with my family that if something really does get me down, I believe that I can call on them; but my first call is often to God. I know that he should always be the first and not just often, but I am learning more and more how to lean and depend on God. I don't have to worry about anyone repeating anything that I have said, nor do I have to wonder how much I can confide in him. I also don't have to put on any fronts. You know how we try to act like we are not hurt and that we are tough and can handle everything that comes our way.

But when it comes to God I can get laid out on the floor, crying, runny nose and all. Sometimes I get all choked up and can't say what it is that has gone wrong with me. I don't have that problem with God because I know that he knows everything about me already and nothing that I can ever do will he hold against me.

Sometimes I can be arguing with my husband and I will try to talk to him and it seems as though he's not understanding or receiving anything I'm saying. So I just stop talking to him and start talking to God. I will start saying things like "God, I know that you see this. I am depending on you, Lord to fix this." Or I will say, "Now Lord, he is your child and Father, I know that you are probably the only one who knows what is going on with him, Lord. Your holy word tells me that we must pray for one another."

This is where it gets crazy. I will say "Now Lord, I am doing my part so Lord can you please fix him because I don't believe that he even knows that he is being used by the enemy. Lord, he is driving me absolutely nuts."

We have this saying at our house when the conversation starts to get a bit heated. One of us will tell the other, "Don't become a willing vessel." This means don't knowingly allow the devil to use you to do his will.

Standing still and waiting for my answer does not work all the time. It is as if I get restless and nothing makes any sense to me. I will keep going over it in my mind whatever the problem may be. The more I think the more I get frustrated and before I know it I will have a four alarm fire going on in my mind. Usually all it turns out to be about is something that someone has said. I don't know why I let it bother me, because most of the time I can hear something and if it isn't true I will smile to myself and keep going ,

I can remember something that my step-mom would say. "If a person is talking about you and you are not talking or thinking about them, then you must be doing something right for them to be calling your name." Sometimes it does hurt, especially when you know that you have been good to a person and for no good reason whatsoever, they will cause your name to be put into something.

So yes, sometimes I will call on this person that I am going to call Pastor N.D. I will call pastor and

I will be knowing that all I need to do is calm down and not pay any attention to what is going on, but somehow it won't sink into my spirit. But when pastor starts to talk He will say "Now sis, how are you doing?" This will open the door for me to spill everything that I was trying to hold. I don't know how pastor knows just what to say, because I will start running off at the mouth as if I have diarrhea at the mouth.

After pastor listens to what I have said then pastor will say to me, "Now sis, what does the word of God say about this? Don't you believe in the word? What is the problem? You have your tools (my Bible); now use them." By now I would start to feel ashamed of myself for letting it get to me in the way that it did. I would then ask for prayer and from there give the full run down on why it didn't work when I tried to pray on my own. It will be like me trying to medicate myself.

Come to find out it will be more than just one thing that will be bothering me in order for me to get so wound up. Some of the time it will often be one of those things that I will have let go on and not have dealt with it and it will end up being the straw that breaks the camel's back. You know what I am talking about. When you tell yourself that now this person has got one more time to do such and such, only for that one more time to have become ten more times.

Sometimes my husband will ask me why I let the things that people do bother me so much. So we started to study this and meditate and pray on it and this went on for about several months until one day

I was looking at myself in the mirror and the answer was always right there in the front of me.

I would let the things bother me because I needed change in my life. I found that this person could have been me and the things that they were doing were some of the very same things that I didn't want in my life any more. So by me seeing them I also saw myself, and I didn't like what it was that I was seeing. So in order for it not to have any effect on me, I needed to make some changes from within. This change bought about growth and a new kind of peace of mind. So now when I hear or see someone doing something that doesn't set well with my spirit, I just say "Thank you Lord… Lord you are worth the changes that I need in my life."

I have learned that in order for me to grow into the likeness of the Godly woman that has been ordained from the beginning of my life, I must let go of all the old things and the old ways of thinking. I know that I can do all things through Christ who strengthens me. But in order for me to bring about a change in my life, first of all I had to unlearn everything that I had been taught about being grown. I didn't know that there was a difference between being grown and being a young woman. You see when you are an adult, you will do whatever you feel is needed to get you from point A to point B. You will convince yourself that it does not matter. We tell ourselves that we are doing these things because everyone else is doing it.

But when we come to the point in our lives when we come to the end of ourselves we find out that our way does not work for our good, and it takes a wise enough person to come to the truth about themselves. It is like we are defeating our own selves; we will walk around in the same circle. Now the foolish person will not notice that they are traveling around in the same circle, but the wiser person will see it and not just see it but do something about it.

Have you ever been in a situation where it seems like you just can't win for losing and you end up having a conversation with yourself saying something like this: "I should have known better than to do that. But how could you have known better when you don't bother to listen to anybody's advice about anything?

Have you ever tried to tell someone something and you knew that it would help them do something much better than the way that they are doing it, only for them to say to you "yeah I know but." It's as if they are saying to you, "Don't tell me anything because I already know everything." When whatever they are doing goes wrong, then they come back to you for your help. This is what I am talking about when I say that we have got to unlearn our old ways of doing things, because everything that we have already learned over the years will only hinder our spiritual walk. You know how we are all trying to get ahead and don't care who we step on trying to get to the top at any cost.

Do you know that if we were to listen to our self all the time, there is no telling what kind of mess we would get into. We have got to get out of our own way. You know it is an awful thing to follow someone else into destruction, but it is even worse to lead yourself into destruction. There is this old saying that I heard long ago and I don't know who it was who said it first but I have used it in my walk in life, and it says, "To dig your own grave is quite a sight, but to bury yourself it's not very bright."

When we realize that there is a better way of doing things, we can get out of self's way and start to become a better person. Now we are changing from being grown into being a young person who has respect for ourselves and others.

Sometimes we will know that there is something wrong in our lives, but we have been burdened with the problem for so long that we start to make excuses for being in the situations. We begin to accept it as a way of life for us and most of the time that way of life will usually be the easy way out.

So please, if you find that you have been stained and that you are not growing in your spiritual walk, it doesn't have to be permanent. If Jesus fixed it for me, I know that he will also do it for you.

I pray that whoever it is that reads this chapter, if you haven't already stepped into that mighty person of God that you have been called to be, that it will happen soon for you.

Be not thou envious against evil men, neither desire to be with them. For their heart studieth destruction, and their lips talk of mischief. Through wisdom is an house builded; and by understanding it is established: And by knowledge shall the chambers be filled with all precious and pleasant riches.
Proverbs 24:1-4

The Lord is my shepherd; I shall not want. He maketh me to lie down in green pastures: he leadeth me beside the still waters. He restoreth my soul: he leadeth me in the paths of righteousness for his name's sake. Yea, though I walk through the valley of the shadow of death, I will fear no evil: for thou art with me; thy rod and thy staff they comfort me. Thou preparest a table before me in the presence of mine enemies: thou anointest my head with oil; my cup runneth over. Surely goodness and mercy shall follow me all the days of my life: and I will dwell in the house of the Lord for ever.

Psalm 23:1-6

CHAPTER 12

God is Good, God is Great!

When I was young I use to always talk to God even though I didn't really know him. As I said earlier, we did go to church just about every Sunday as children. All we did was go to church, and I can say for myself that I didn't have an idea or understanding of what church was about or who and what God was to me.

We did what was expected of us: show up and sit and listen to what the preacher man was talking about for three to four hours. We use to catch it trying to stay awake. I couldn't understand why in church it would take everything that I could think of to stay awake but as soon as church was over I was wide awake. It was hard trying to act as if I were paying any attention while in church. If someone had told me that they would give me a million dollars to tell them the topic for the sermon of the day, I wouldn't be able to tell them.

Sometimes someone would tell one of us to do something and we would just do it. A lot of the time we didn't know why we were doing whatever it was that we were asked to do, all we knew was that the sooner we did it the sooner that it would be over. I know that this may seem crazy, but nobody ever said to us "Let me explain to you what this means and why it is that we do it."

Week after week, year after year we would come to church, line up and come in trying not to sit too close to the front. We would fight to see who got to sit at the end of the benches because whoever got there was able to prop their head on the arm rail and get comfortable enough to go to sleep. The only bad part about this was that it was always an older person or an usher right behind us and they would thump us on the back of the head and tell us to straighten up.

We were too dumb to realize that the arm rail was a trap. If we still went back to sleep, the next thing that we got was pinched on the back of our necks. Somehow my step-mom had gotten to all the adults and had given them permission to beat us if it was necessary.

Somehow we always ended up in church without her, but come to think of it she would hardly ever be there in church with us. She would always get all of us dressed for church and then she would drop us off at church and leave us there. She would tell us that she was going back home and get dressed and come back. Sometimes she would and sometimes she wouldn't. When she didn't come back we knew to catch a ride back with our aunt and her family.

My step-mom would ask the other church members to please make sure that we didn't act up in church. If we did, she told them to not waste any of their time trying to talk to us. She gave them permission to do whatever they needed to do to get us back in line. And she told them to make sure that they let her know so that she could whip us again when we got home, and they would do just that.

Whenever we acted out in church, a hand would be coming at us from every direction. We never knew who was watching us. The ushers and those old ladies would pinch us so hard. You could not holler or cry because that meant that you wanted to be taken outside. Lord, help us if that were to happen because you would get dragged out and everyone would turn around to give you an evil eye. Now, isn't that just the nuttiest thing that you have ever heard? Who would believe the saints were sitting right in church giving folks the evil eye.

So now our feet were dangling in the air and we were going to the place where us kids liked to call no man's land. The grown-ups would take us far enough away from the church so the adult could curse and beat the fool out of us and no one in the church could hear them.

Now this is the part that always got me. They are beating us and the whole time they will be telling us to shut up, or they will say something even crazier like "If you don't be quiet I will give you something to really cry about." I would be saying, well, if you punching the mess out of me, is that not enough to be crying about. Then I really do need to know just what is it that I can cry about. I said this to myself

because I might not have been the brightest crayon
in the box, but I promise you this, I wasn't far from
being the brightest. I like to think of myself as being
the next in line for being the brightest.

So now that my head is back on straight and I am
no longer seeing two of everything, the grown up
will have the nerve to say "Go in the bath room and
wash your face to help wake you up," Then again I
will say, "Are you for real? Wash my face to wake
up, don't you think that smack and punch was
enough to wake me up? So what if I just go in the
bath room and wash off the blood from that busted
lip you just gave me or maybe I should try to wash
off your hand print from the side of my face." But as
I said earlier, I said this to myself. Why on earth
would I want to be awake to hear another word that
the preacher was talking about?

This man was so boring that he would be reading
from his notes and ask the congregation if anyone
knew where he was at, because he had lost his place
where he was reading from, and this is no lie. This
man would put his own self to sleep. We would
watch him to see how long he would act as if he was
closing his eyes trying to think of something, when
he knew very well that he was snoozing himself.
Sometimes he would be saying something and he
would start to stutter and scratch his head and the
next thing you know he would be gone for a moment
or two. Then he would open his eyes and say, "Wow,
I really wish that you guys could see what the Lord
just showed me," and again I would have to have a
little conversation with myself and say, "I have seen
it too, but I was so rudely awaken from my dream."

I could not believe my ears. He was using the Lord's name and knew that he was lying, and the older church folks would be falling for that mess. You could tell that they were buying it because they would say, "Thank you Lord for dealing with our pastor." Those nuts even had the audacity to say that other churches would do anything to get our pastor. I can't believe that they were so gullible cause if it was up to me they could have that cat, because I was tired of getting smacked around because of him being so boring and putting me to sleep anyways.

Can you believe that the mothers of the church had the nerve to call him a gifted man of God? Yeah, he was gifted alright. His gift was putting folks to sleep. Why was it okay for the older church folks to nod off to sleep and nothing was ever said to them? It was talked about, but not to them.

I believed that if I talked to God long enough that sooner or later he would answer and say something. I use to believe that because I didn't get what I was asking for, the answer must be "no." You can imagine that I got a lot of no's from God. I not only wanted to believe in God but I kind of needed to believe in him. I had heard so many times in church about this God.

Basically the way that I understand it was that God owns everything and if you ask him for anything he would do it for you. I understood that our church was God's house. So I figured this much out. Hey, I go to his house every week and even though I had not yet seen him I could remember hearing the preacher say that God was there so he had to have seen me, even if I hadn't seen him.

Maybe he came when I had fallen asleep, but he had to have seen me being dragged out of church for being asleep. So why should I waste any time asking and being turned down by the middle man when I could go straight to the owner and ask for what I wanted. So I thought that I needed to get to know the head man who was and is in charge. You know that if someone speaks to you every day, sooner or later, you will remember them. Back in those days I needed to know someone in high places. Because whoever it was that was supposed to be looking out for me wasn't on their job. So I took it upon myself to look out for myself.

I find it amazing that even though I didn't have a good relationship with the Lord and didn't know him, I knew about him. I don't understand it but I can recall thinking, if it is true that God has made me, then I am not a mistake and nor am I junk, because God doesn't make junk.

As far back as I can remember, I heard about God and his will for mankind, that everybody was put here on earth for a reason, that we only needed to find out what his plan is for us and then all would be well. For a long time I believed that I was put here only for the purpose of suffering and causing misery to others. There was not a day that went by that I wasn't told that my step-mom's life would have been a lot better off without me. Let her tell it, I was good at causing pain, so this is why I believed that this was my calling in life.

As I got older I found out that it wasn't me that was the one who brought on so much suffering in our family. Turns out it was my step-mom because after she put me out of her house for the last time at the age of 18 (I never did go back), I would hear other family members saying how much mess she was always causing for everyone that she came in contact with. Either she would say anything she felt like saying to people or she would repeat something she heard someone else say. She called it "speaking her mind." Either way whenever you saw her, if you knew what was good for you, you would turn and go the other way. Believe me some of them did this only for her to go to another person and tell them a whole different story about why they didn't want to see her. She didn't only get on people's nerves she also made people sick. Have you ever heard someone say that "you make me sick," yep, she was that person.

I don't know why but I was always the type of person who didn't go over to anyone's house. The only way for a person to be able to say that they had seen me was if they came over to where I lived or they would see me as I was out in the streets taking care of my business. I have always been a home-body and not a busy-body.

I bet you that if my step-mom would have known that she was doing something good for me by putting me out of her house that she would have thought twice about it. Getting put out made me get my own place, which also meant that I didn't have to see or be around her any longer. I had a place that I could go to and have peace of mind. I had never before in my whole life experienced such peace before. I didn't even know how to act. I was like a freed slave.

When I had to go grocery shopping, I had never done it before, so I didn't know that to fry chicken I needed to buy a frying pan, some cooking oil, some seasoning and flour. I didn't even have a fork to turn the chicken over or a plate to put it on after cooking it.

I was lost, but I loved it. I had to learn how to cook different foods other than just chicken. That's all I cooked the first month. I was like Forest Gimp with all the different ways to cook scrimp. I went through all the different ways there were to cook chicken. The reason that I was cooking so much chicken was because I worked in a chicken factory and got a discount on cases of it, and we didn't have to pay for it at that moment but the following week the company would take the money out of our pay checks. And there was a lot of chicken that came in those boxes.

I had eaten so much chicken that I thought that I was turning into a big chicken. It felt so good not to have to be around all that cursing. Getting slapped around along with all of the other stress and pain was over.

For the first time in my life I was free. I remember thinking to myself that the whole thing was just a dream, and that eventually I would awake from the dream and I would still be there in her house. Sometimes I would just walk around not being able to believe the freedom or the quietness and the peacefulness at this moment and time of my life. I could actually picture myself as Adam was walking in the noon day with God talking in the Garden of Eden. It was something that I had never experienced before in my life and if newness was a word to describe my feelings then I just felt like a new person.

Sometimes I would find myself just sitting and waiting to see if someone was going to come and say to me "Hey, you are not suppose to be here." Nothing this good had ever happened to me before and I didn't know how to handle it. I remember one day my dad came over and said, "Do you know before you use to look much older then you really are, but now you look like you have lost at least five or more years off your life."

I couldn't believe how well I was feeling. It was like I had just been taught how to breathe. To me this new freedom was worth more to me than anything that I had ever known. Little did I know that there was going to come a time when I was going to have to fight for that very same freedom.

After about a month or so my step sister started to come around. She told me my step-mom had plans to try and have me evicted from my new place. The lady that I was renting from came by and told me my step-mom was trying to cause problems for her. She had rented me her place without going to my step-mom first. My step-mom told her that if she had stayed out of her business that I would have had to come back to her.

My step-mom had a reputation of trying to be bad, and everybody that knew her knew that she liked to run things, but this new rent lady was not from around there; she also came with a reputation and if you were to bark at her, she did more than bark back. If you tried to push her around you might just find out that she was not going to be moved so easily. When I tell you that this woman didn't take no mess, my step-mom could not handle her like she did everybody else, and she couldn't stand it. Before long everyone was talking about there was a new sheriff in town and that my step-mom had found her match. Around our neighborhood it was like there was a big fight or a big event was coming to town.

All I know was that this woman was standing up for me and I was not going to let her down. I did all that I could do to fight for myself. I had never stood up for myself before and I ended up learning a lot from this new land-Lord. She was tough and went after what she wanted and I wanted to be just like her.

After my step-mom found out that she couldn't handle this lady she started on me. She had someone come and knock down my front door, and that didn't work. Then she had someone to break into my car at work and take the steering wheel off. That didn't work. She sent the police to my house and said that I was not taking care of my little girl, and that didn't work. Then she went to the school and picked up my daughter without my permission and that didn't work either.

This crazy woman saw me walking one day, and tried to run me down, and this is what worked. My father told me that I needed to leave town because he had been hearing some of the things that my step-mom had been saying that she was going to do to me. He finally had enough of what she was doing so I don't know who called who but my dad had made arrangements for me to leave town.

It was hard for me since I had really never been on my own like this before. I asked my father why we couldn't just call the law on her, and the only thing that he said was "No, because you were never suppose to have been here this long any way." I didn't understand what it was that he was saying, but I could feel the pain in his voice as he told me to just do what I have to do and maybe one day things would get better for me.

Before I could get on the bus to leave town, my father said to me that if I could find it inside of me whenever this whole mess was straighten out maybe it would be a year from now or ten years from now he wanted to know if I could forgive him for stealing my life and my happiness.

This was the last time that I saw my father strong and rugged as he was in the prime of his life. The next time I got to see my father he had throat cancer, high blood pressure, diabetes and his stomach had been removed because of some kind of cancer. I don't know what all it was that he had. But I do know that the last time that I saw him he was so weak and frail.

"This is it for me, baby girl. Now I have done my part for you. Now I am finished; my job is done."

My dad told me he didn't believe he did his job that well, but nevertheless his job for me was done. I didn't know what he meant. I thought he was mad at me because he kept saying the same thing to me.

"Baby girl, your daddy is washing his hands with you so don't you ever come back here, because I won't be here for you."

As I got back on the bus, I cried because I thought that he didn't want to see me anymore. I didn't know that he was dying. I never got to say goodbye and I didn't get to tell him that I finally do understand what he was talking about, and yes, I do forgive him and I have learned how to love him even more than ever.

It took many years before I really did understand what he was trying to do for me. I think that out of all the years of me knowing my father that this was the hardest thing that he ever had to do. As I sit here today I can remember hearing him say that out of all of his children I was the only one who had deep roots with him, and that I would be the one who made his heart hurt the most.

I really do thank the Lord for blessing me with the gift of forgiving and to be able to see this journey through, so when I say that God is good, God is great this is not just a grace that I learned as a little kid; it is the stepping stone that I have been blessed with to be able to stand on even when I didn't have a foot of my own to stand on.

Some people are born with a silver spoon in their mouth, but I was born with a solid rock to be able to stand. No matter how many times I'm knocked down, I don't have to stay down because not only does this rock guide my footsteps, it also elevates me higher then I could ever imagine being. So now I am able to look down and pull someone else up with me.

For when we were yet without strength,
in due time Christ died for the ungodly.
For scarcely for a righteous man will one die: yet
peradventure for a good man some would even
dare to die. But God commended his love toward
us, in that, while we were yet sinners, Christ died
for us. Much more then, being now justified by his
blood, we shall be saved from wrath through him.
Romans 5:6-9

In the beginning was the Word, and the Word was with God and the Word was God. The same was in the beginning with God.
All things were made by him; and without him was not anything made that was made. In him was life; and the life was the light of men. And the light shined in darkness; and the darkness comprehended it not.
John 1:1-5

CHAPTER

Life is Good after All

Before I finish this book I want to be sure that I didn't start this project complaining and also ended it the same way. I do not want you to believe that I started out lost and all alone and ended by still being lost and alone.

To tell you the truth God has really been good to me; he has been better to me than I have been to myself. Every time I turn around, the Lord is blessing me. I know that you probably have heard this before but I was headed down the path of destruction and death. I didn't like myself and for such a long time I believed that I was the ugliest thing that ever lived. After hearing this for years and even decades I started to believe it. Truthfully, I never could envision good things happening to me or for me. When a young person has been brainwashed for so many years, and has been told that she will never amount to anything and that her life is a waste as much as I was told this, how can anything else in life matter.

Tell me, how do you hope to become something better, when you are taught to think of yourself as less than nothing? How does a person that is so damaged within even hope for something better.

When I was coming up even as a small child we were taught that if you have something that is too rotten then you must cut it until you find a good part, but if it is rotten throughout out then you must throw it away. This is what I believed about myself. I didn't come to this conclusion on my own. I had been told this pretty much all of my childhood.

During the entire time I was in school, I can truthfully say there was only one teacher who told me I could become somebody special. She told me that if I stayed in school and worked hard that folks would be happy to be able to say that they knew me. I wasn't old enough to know what she was telling me because I was only about five or six years old. So, I didn't know what she meant by this. All I could get out of this was how does a person stay in school.

I didn't have any plans on leaving school. I thought maybe she is telling me to flunk my grade or something. One year in grade school for career day I can remember one of my teachers asking our class what would we like to become when we grew up. One little girl said that she wanted to become a nurse and another girl just wanted to learn everything that she could learn so that whenever someone would say to her that she thought that she knew everything then it would be true. One boy who was the class clown said he wanted to become a bum; he didn't feel that there was any need for him to continue on going to school. In fact he believed that he might have learned too much and this would make him over qualified.

When it was my turn all I could come up with was that I only wanted to be left alone. For saying this, my teacher told me that I was headed down the road for nothing good in life. So here was not only my family members telling me this but now this teacher is telling me the same exact thing. The bad part about this was that she (the teacher) had told our whole class to not worry about being graded for our answers so we must try our best to answer as truthfully as possible. So even though this was my heart's desire and I was being as truthful as I could be, my choice for my life was not accepted.

Could I ever dream of something bigger and better in life when what I already was, wasn't good enough for anyone else?

As I sit here I can remember one day when I was just about to turn nine or ten years old, and my father asked me "Girl how many friends do you have?", and I said that I didn't know.

"What on earth do you mean you don't know? This is how you can tell if you are a likeable person. When you talk, is everyone listening or is no one listening?. If you have a lot of friends then you are a big liar; either you are telling your own lies or you are telling someone else's lies. People don't hang around to hear the truth; they only want to hear lies. Now if you don't have many friends then I guess you are a person who tells the truth."

Then my father asked: "What do you have to say about this fact of life?"

"Well, dad, I guess that makes you really smart or either it means you are really dumb."

"What is that supposed to mean?", he asked.

"If you know this and you found this out all by yourself then what makes you think that someone else hasn't thought of this also, so now everybody knows that you are a big story teller (back then us kids were not allowed to say the word lie)."

My father started to laugh and told me to watch my mouth cause if he didn't know any better he would think that I was calling him a liar.

So now back to what I was saying, how does a person look forward to life when all of their past they have only wanted to die? So I could do one of two things and that was to either lie and tell my teacher and classmates what I thought it was that they wanted to hear, or I could tell them the truth which nobody wanted to hear. It is a sad day when a young child has to learn how to play the game of life. But I have heard that if it does not kill you it will only make you stronger. But this seemed funny to me because I didn't feel any stronger and I wasn't dead, so I guess this saying was a lie.

I never knew that some of the things that we learn as a child would turn out to be what saves us as an adult. I remember how hard it was for me to learn how to say my grace and I really did catch it trying to learn my prayers at night. I didn't know what the word of God said about giving thanks for everything; I just thought that this was something that my step-mom used to make us say.

I guess all of this time she has been taking credit for something that God has been saying from the very beginning of time. I wonder if my step-mom knows that God is not pleased with this. No matter how bad life may have seemed back in my past, today has really been good for me. The one true saying that I have learned for my day to day walk is "Hold on to God's unchanging hands." You see, we are the ones who change. God is immutable; he never changes.

We must stop taking credit for God's victory in our life. Have you ever noticed that whenever something goes wrong in our lives the first thing that we want to do is give it to the Lord for him to fix it. But when something good happens we want to keep it and get all of the glory for something that we didn't even do, because God has done it. We don't give him the praises and the glory; this is what belongs to God, not all of our troubles and mishaps.

We are so quick to blame everyone else for the trouble that we get ourselves into. We will say that my spouse caused me to do this or maybe it was our children who were the reason that it happened. Or it was because of my job or my boss who is at fault. And this is the number one person who is the cause of our wrong doings: the devil made me do it.

We need to stop telling lies to everyone and even ourselves. The devil can't make you or I or anyone else do anything. The only thing that the devil can do is to influence us or show us something in our minds. It is up to us to either turn away from it or to go on ahead and do what has been presented to us. The devil cannot put any action into work on our behalf; it is only by our own will power that we put it into works.

We have a choice in life to do the right thing or to do the wrong things. We have the ability to do well, but it is in our nature to choose to do the wrong thing, and most of the time the wrong thing is most often the easy thing to do.

We choose to believe that the right things that we should do are the hardest things to do, but it will only seem this way because we have not trained ourselves to take the time out and just do it right from the beginning. You know that I have heard that the wrong way may be the quickest and the easiest way to get something done, but I am here to share with you that quickness and easy often times turn out to be the messiest. And you will have to spend double the amount of time fixing the mess that you have made, when all you have to do from the start is to do it the right way and be done with it.

When we choose to do the right things in life and we get ourselves in the habit of doing it, it starts to become natural for us and we don't have to think twice about it. In fact when we train ourselves to do what is right then our children will see it and learn from seeing us doing what is right. Their classmates will in return see it and they will pick up on it and from there take it home and so on. Yes, it does start with one person. And, yes, we can make this world a better place.

As the years go by I have learned how to be responsible for my own actions; it took me many years to learn this. I learned from my childhood whenever something bad happened, the only safe place was not to be at fault. It was best to not be anywhere around.

Because my step-mom would call herself trying to be wise by just coming into a room and beating everybody that was around where the trouble was. She said that this way she knew that she had beat the right person, and if you were one of the persons who was not to blame then she felt that she had just whipped you for something that she didn't know about. Or the beating that you just received was for something that you were going to do. So in her mind she felt justified for just being a bully and just beating up on kids.

You know she might have been bright in skin color but she wasn't very bright in the brains department. So whenever something would go wrong the first thing that we learned to say was it wasn't me, mama. Even in school I had learned to say it wasn't me, even though it was me some of the time. I knew that in order to get out of trouble one must learn how to holler the loudest, and sometimes it worked and a lot of times it didn't work.

This was like the card in the monopoly games, you know, the get out of jail free card. I had learned the hard way that if I would tell the truth that it didn't matter because my step-mom still wouldn't believe me. I started to tell lies right from the very start, and do you know that the more I lied the more my step-mom seemed to believe me and the more that I would tell her the truth the less she would believe me so I just started telling her what she wanted to hear, and from there I started blaming everyone for everything that went wrong in my life.

This became a hard habit for me to break because for years I would see everyone else doing

things and whenever they got caught it was never
their fault. Someone else was always the blame. My
father did it so much that he would say that it wasn't
him and if you would tell him that you saw him
doing wrong, he would tell you that if you didn't
come up to him and put your hand on him then it
wasn't him. Listening to him tell it, everyone has a
twin somewhere and his twin always showed up
when something wrong was going down. But if it
turned out to be something good then guess what,
that was him who was doing it and everyone that I
knew would always say that someone else was the
cause of them being in the trouble.

I can't ever remember hearing one of them say,
"Yes I did it and it is my fault." Because no one was
ever at fault this meant that nobody had to ever say I
am wrong and for this I am sorry. So this is why it
was such a great problem for me when I did start to
seek Christ Jesus to come into my life. I needed to
first confess my sins and I knew that God already
knew my faults. I had to own up to them all one by
one, and for so many of years it was always
somebody else who did it. That's when I needed to
'fess up and say it was and is me. Just by saying
those words it has changed my whole life; life has
never   been
the same.

I don't worry about people anymore because
they cannot do any harm to me any longer, and all I
can see now is how can I be pleasing in God's sight.
I can and do forgive other people for the hurt and the
pain and the suffering that I went through. Because
the past is just what it says; it has passed and there is

nothing that I can do to change it. Because yesterday is gone and tomorrow may never be mine, I must make today stand for something. Life is funny. You can live your whole life trying to do good and one day you can do something wrong. One day and this one day of wrong doing will outweigh your whole life of good deeds.

Now the new me will stand up and say what's on my mind. I no longer hide or hang my head low because I love me and so does Jesus. To me that's top shelf quality love and I will not accept anything less.

When I find out that a person does not like me it doesn't bother me and that don't stop me from liking and loving me. So when I mess up, I will say please forgive me and I am wrong. I know how to fess up. But I also have learned how to speak up for me. If someone does or says something I don't go run and tell someone else. I know how to talk for me and I have found out that if I leave it alone and let God handle it he will fix it like no one else can. I no longer will accept less in life nor will I let anyone else throw their trash on me. I will hold my head up high; I don't try to be no more or less then what God has called me to be.

I know that every day is not going to be sunshine, that there is going to be some cloudy days and even some storms, but I can handle it. I know that I will not break. I am strong and I've got God on my side, and this means that all things are possible.

I have learned not to worry about things that I cannot control and because of this I am able to sleep at night. And I don't stress over the problems of the world because the world is a messed up place and if we don't stop to catch our breath it will be too late. And beside all of that, life is just too short to be living here on earth in hell and then end up dying and going to hell, too.

We must learn how to put things in order, which is God first and then self and my family. I say self next because if we don't take care of self then who will and we need to stop robbing ourselves. There is nothing wrong with having nice clothes and a nice car to drive and we can go out for dinner sometimes. This is why we work - to buy a home or to go back to school for higher learning in order to get a better paying job. It's call investing in one's self.

As I said earlier if we don't then who will? You can't get a loan from anyone nowadays, not the bank or our family. We can't go to our friends because our friends are doing the same thing that we are doing and that is trying to make ends meet, and God forbid if you do find someone who will lend you some money whether it is a bank or a grant. Now the real problems start. You no longer work for self anymore; now you work for the lender because if you are late with their money you will lose everything that you have. When we borrow from lenders we not only have to pay back what we borrowed but we have to pay for the loan as well and pray that we are not late with the payment. Now we start to lose sleep at night and stress starts to catch up with us and from there our health becomes a problem and now there is no peace of mind. So I have learned to do what I can and not to worry about the rest.

Next thing in line that we must look out for is trying to please other people. We will never be able to please everybody. And never will we have everyone's support when we are trying to better ourselves. We have to start looking to God for our support and then our family.

I once heard a person say that a man can work from sun to sun, but a woman's work is never done. Now I am not saying that our men don't work hard because that would not be true. God has blessed me with a husband who will work all day and then come home and get ready for church and come home again and fall asleep while eating his dinner, and then get up and do it all again the next day. So I am not saying that our men don't work hard, but there are some women that I know who work hard. From the time her feet hits the floor, she is on the run. She is working, cleaning, cooking, and dealing with the kids and other family members. Life is hard and for all of the single mothers out there my hat is off to you. I don't know how you do it, but keep on doing what it is that you are doing because in the end you will receive everything that you have been working so hard for.

I know that there are some single fathers out there as well, please don't think that the world don't see you because we do and we are proud of you. So keep your head up and know that your help is near. There is a reward set aside just for you because you are a dying breed. I know that for whatever the reason you are raising your kids alone, you are going to be blessed in the end; you will pass great wisdom on to your sons, and this will make whomever that seeks to be his wife a very blessed woman. So from me to you look up to the hills from which cometh your help which is God all mighty. Yes, weeping may endure for a night but joy comes in the morning.

I would like for this chapter to be in memory of my family and love ones who are no longer here. They are gone but not forgotten ...

Rest in peace Ms. J.J.; Mr. W.L.O.; Ms. L.B.P.; Mr. C.Y.; Mr. J.J.; Mr. C.S.; Mr. F.E.; T.J.; B.J.; Mr. A.J.; Ms. T.L.M.; and the list goes on.

Gone much too soon.

Know you not that ye are the temple of God, and
that the spirit of God dwelled in you?
If any man defile the temple of God,
him shall God destroy; for the temple of
God is holy, which temple ye are.
1Corinthians 3:16-17

Letter to the Reader

Dear Reader,

I am honored that you have read this book. As a writer and avid reader, I have been helped tremendously by inspirational books that I have read. These books have helped me tremendously. First and foremost is the Holy Bible.

I spend quiet times writing notes to myself, sometimes for church and other times for school. Frequently God will bless me with a daily thought. Occasionally, the thoughts become a poem or a song. There are times when I write to get my mind and spirit on the same page.

Initially, my memory would fail me with some of the thoughts I was blessed with; therefore, I find it necessary now to write down my thoughts with the time and date. I have written something and came back to it after a certain passage of time and wondered who wrote it. Later I would come across an additional part of that same writing and realize that I wrote it.

It seems as though God has always been sending me whispers of encouragement throughout my whole life. Believe me when I tell you this, I have had a relationship with the Lord as far back as I can remember. It seems kind of funny now when I look back. Thank you, Jesus!

You know how it is when you first start to piece a puzzle together and you have no picture to look at to get a clue about what the finished puzzle should look like. That is what was happening to me. God would be sending me in a certain direction while assuring me of his presence. I simply had to seek him for all things.

I always talked to God even though I did not know how to wait and listen. I thought he didn't hear me. I believed that God didn't have time for me and didn't care for me. As a child I thought that maybe he was only a God for the grown-ups with no time for kids.

But today with more pieces of my life's puzzle, I can see a better picture. Now when I look back, I can see that every time I called on him, He heard and answered. Sometimes he even sent someone there for me.

In fact, He loved me so much that he sent his only begotten son to die for me. That is awesome! Do you know anyone else who would do that for you? I don't. This is the kind of God I serve. Just think! Jesus laid down his life for me.

Dear readers, I can only say God is good.

But to God be the glory. I have learned of his grace and his mercy. I had to get to know him for myself. I pray that you will get to know him if you have not already done so.

I want to thank everyone who reads this book and say to you that God does not make mistakes. No matter how bad things may look now, I promise you if you will just hold on a bit longer you, too, will have a story of your very own that you can share with other readers.

Please allow me to share my personal keys of spiritual wisdom with you.

Keys of Spiritual Wisdom

1) Pray three or more times a day.
2) Maintain a direct communication with the Lord.
3) Learn how to worship God, the Father.
4) Study and read the Word of God daily.
5) Learn to watch what I say and do.
6) Be reasonable for my actions, as well as my thoughts.
7) Respect others, and always show Godly love.
8) Meditate on the Word daily.
9) Try to learn something new daily.
10) Pray for others without ceasing.
11) Look for the good in all things.
12) Always remember that I am more than a conquerer.
13) Always stay lined up with the Word of God.
14) Try to keep all vows.
15) Do all that I can to be a blessing to others.
16) Keep the Lord's commandments.
17) Always ask for God's forgiveness.
18) Learn to always forgive one another, and keep lifting each other up.
19) Try not to tear anyone down.
20) Daily worship and praise God.
21) Never steal or try to share God's glory with another.
22) Learn how to be a humble and Godly person.
23) Never take credit for anything; to God be the glory at all times.
24) Always remember that God owes me nothing, but it is I who owe God everything.
25) Always serve the Lord with meekness and joy.

26)   I must always pay my tithes.
27)   Always know that I am covered by the blood of Jesus.
28)   I must sift out the things that I see and hear.
29)   I must give birth to my dreams.
30)   I must never lose sight of the prize.

I pray that these words that I have shared with you will encourage you. And maybe you can extract something from this that will help you to continue on your walk in life. And to God be the glory always.

Yours in Christ,
Caroline Judd

www.ingramcontent.com/pod-product-compliance
Lightning Source LLC
Chambersburg PA
CBHW051959090426
42741CB00008B/1466